Emotional Intelligence & Cognitive Behavioral Therapy + Hygge

(5 Book Box Set)

Ryan James & Amy White

Table of Contents

Book #1 – Emotional Intelligence: Definitive Guide

Chapter 1: Introduction to Emotional Intelligence 7
Chapter 2: Difference between Intelligence Quotient and Emotional Quotient 20
Chapter 3: Benefits of Emotional Intelligence 25
Chapter 4: Proven Tips to Boost Your Emotional Intelligence 32
Conclusion 48

Book #2 – Emotional Intelligence: Definitive Guide

Introduction 52
Chapter 1: Understanding the Purpose of Emotions 55
Chapter 2: Increasing Your Own Self-Awareness 59
Chapter 3: Reducing Negative habits 63
Chapter 4: Stress Management 67
Chapter 5: The "Bounce Back" Effect 71
Chapter 6: Expressing Complex Emotions 75
Chapter 7: Handling Intimacy 80
Chapter 8: Managing Your Reactions 84
Chapter 9: Emotions in Others 88
Chapter 10: Taking Responsibility: Taking Control 91
Conclusion 94

Book #3 – Cognitive Behavioral Therapy

Introduction 98
Chapter 1: From Forests to the Urban Sprawl 100
Chapter 2: Understanding Depression 109
Chapter 3: The Intersection of Anxiety and Depression 115
Chapter 4: Things You Can Do Today 117
Chapter 5: Things You Can Do Tomorrow 125
Chapter 6: Looking to Your Future 132
Conclusion 136

Book #4 – Cognitive Behavioral Therapy Mastery

Introduction 141
Chapter 1: A Brief Look at cognitive behavioral therapy 142
Chapter 2: Multimodal Therapy 145
Chapter 3: Looking at Reality 150
Chapter 4: Acceptance and Commitment 154
Chapter 5: Functional Analytics 158
Chapter 6: Cognitive Processing 162
Chapter 7: Reprocessing and EMDT 166
Chapter 8: Rational Therapy Method 170
Chapter 9: Dialectical Therapy 174
Conclusion 178

Book #5 – Hygge

Introduction 182
Chapter 1: What is Hygge and How Did It Evolve? 184
Chapter 2: Hygge and Happiness 188
Chapter 3: Tips on How to Make Your Home More Hygge 193
Chapter 4: Prioritizing the People in Your Life Properly 198
Chapter 5: Finding the Food and Hygge Balance 202
Chapter 6: Indulging and Investing in Yourself 207
Chapter 7: Activities with Friends that Are So Hygge it Hurts 212
Chapter 8: Hygge Fashion Tips that Will Make Your Wardrobe Pop 216
Conclusion 220

Emotional Intelligence

The Definitive Guide to Understanding Your Emotions, How to Improve Your EQ and Your Relationships

© Copyright 2017 by Ryan James - All rights reserved.

The following Book is reproduced below with the goal of providing information that is as accurate and as reliable as possible. Regardless, purchasing this Book can be seen as consent to the fact that both the publisher and the author of this book are in no way experts on the topics discussed within, and that any recommendations or suggestions made herein are for entertainment purposes only. Professionals should be consulted as needed before undertaking any of the action endorsed herein.

This declaration is deemed fair and valid by both the American Bar Association and the Committee of Publishers Association and is legally binding throughout the United States.

Furthermore, the transmission, duplication or reproduction of any of the following work, including precise information, will be considered an illegal act, irrespective whether it is done electronically or in print. The legality extends to creating a secondary or tertiary copy of the work or a recorded copy and is only allowed with express written consent of the Publisher. All additional rights are reserved.

The information in the following pages is broadly considered to be a truthful and accurate account of facts, and as such any inattention, use or misuse of the information in question by the reader will render any resulting actions solely under their purview. There are no scenarios in which the publisher or the original author of this work can be in any fashion deemed liable for any hardship or damages that may befall them after undertaking information described herein.

Additionally, the information found on the following pages is intended for informational purposes only and should thus be considered, universal. As befitting its nature, the information presented is without assurance regarding its continued validity or interim quality. Trademarks that mentioned are done without written consent and can in no way be considered an endorsement from the trademark holder.

Chapter 1: Introduction to Emotional Intelligence

There's no escaping the concept of emotional intelligence in today's age. It has suddenly gained a massive momentum everywhere from large corporations to relationship counseling to schools and government agencies. Emotional intelligence is the new psychological health buzzword, and with good reason. It defines your emotional health and interpersonal skills, which are so vital for everyday existence.

The popular phrase was first coined by researchers Peter Salavoy and John Mayer. However, it became popular only in 1996 when researcher-psychologist Dan Goleman published a book titled, *Emotional Intelligence*. So what exactly is the concept of emotional intelligence and why is it such a clinching factor when it comes to choosing people for crucial roles and leading fulfilling personal relationships? Why is everyone feverishly looking for people with a high emotional quotient?

Emotional intelligence as described by Yale psychologist Peter Salovey and John Mayer from the University of New Hampshire is an understanding of one's emotions, empathy for other's feelings and "regulation of emotion in a manner that enhances living." This concept was shortened to make the theory more chewable and interesting for lay people by Harvard psychologist and New York Times writer Daniel Goleman. His book *Emotional Intelligence* complied years of behavioral research on processing feelings. He broadened the definition of smartness, and sought to establish that brainpower, which is measured by standardized IQ tests may not matter as much as mental qualities when it came to predicting a person's overall life success.

Goleman focused on the practical applications and how organizations can use this information to hire the right candidates, how couples could increase their chances of enjoying lasting relationships, how parents could help raise better children and how educational institutions could teach children more effectively.

Emotional Intelligence is the power to be aware of and recognize your emotions. It is the ability to correctly decipher your emotions and the impact they have on others around you. It is also about how you perceive the emotions of those around you and a high understanding about their feelings, which allows you to be a part of more fulfilling relationships.

In his path breaking book, Daniel Goleman focused on five predominant elements within the emotional intelligence framework, including self awareness, self regulation, motivation, empathy and social skills. Thus, emotional intelligence is an evolved understanding/awareness of not just your emotions but also those of others around you to manage relationships more effectively. No surprise then that emotional intelligence has overtaken other attributes such as skills, knowledge, and intelligence quotient when it comes to job recruitments. Everyone wants people with greater understanding, empathy and social skills to forge stronger relationships.

According to Daniel Goleman's blog, the concept of EQ or Emotional Quotient as a phrase is recognized in diverse languages including, German, Korean, Portuguese and Chinese. There's also a mention of religious scholars from diverse faiths communicating with the author to reinforce how the concept of emotional intelligence or emotional quotient echoes their faith's teachings. Hence, emotional intelligence can be all encompassing. It can be applied to various spheres of your life to gain more physical, mental and spiritual nourishment.

While conventional IQ attempts to evaluate a person's capacity to learn information, EQ is about a person's ability to deal with others effectively. Emotional quotient focused on evaluating soft skills such as managing relationships, showing empathy, self-awareness and social awareness. The human brain is understandably complex and it is impossible to asses a person's success quotient based on a single type of intelligence. Therefore, while IQ evaluates your technical prowess within the field of work, EQ helps you with greater emotional awareness of yourself and others.

There is absolutely no correlation between your IQ and EQ score. Some people possess an excellent academic aptitude yet struggle with handling their and other people's emotions. Haven't we all seen folks who are incredibly brainy, yet are clueless when it comes to dealing with people. IQ and EQ evaluate different types of human intelligence. While the former attempts to measure your cognitive prowess, the latter measures your emotional awareness.

Have you been so overtaken by your emotions that you regretted something you said or did later? Few people can deny this. The fact of the matter is, all of us need emotional intelligence in our everyday lives. We can all benefit from learning to manage our emotions more productively. Emotional quotient helps you forge deeper connections with friends and work associates. It leads to higher interpersonal relationship satisfaction, work performance and the ability to control stressful situations.

A heightened emotional quotient gives you the ability to identify and regulate not just your emotions but also those of others. You have no trouble empathizing with people and being aware of their responses. Emotional quotient awards you the power to manage relationships more productively, even in stressful and conflict laden situations.

Let us take an example to illustrate the concept of emotional intelligence. Ron and Bob both had a big fight with their supervisor at work. Ron didn't possess high emotional intelligence, while Bob was emotionally intelligent. On getting home, Ron began cursing and yelling at his kids who were playing noisily in the house. He acted without thinking about the impact his behavior would have on the kids.

On the other hand, when Bob returned home, he noticed his children playing nosily but told himself that they were simply being kids and doing what they do every day. They were not responsible for his problems with his supervisor or how he was feeling at the moment. Why should they be at the receiving end of his feelings when they have nothing to do with it? This is how Bob rationalizes and maintains his calm.

Did you spot the differences in approach in both these instances? Emotionally intelligent people identify their emotions, give it a good thought before reacting and behave in a more emotionally matured manner. They tend to process their emotions mentally before reacting in haste, and regretting it later, which is a typical sign of low emotional intelligence. People with low emotional intelligence react first and think about their reactions later, while people with higher emotional intelligence think before reacting.

Let us see how emotional intelligence can be practiced in some scenarios we are often confronted with. For instance, your best friend asks you for your opinion about his/her new romantic partner whom you thoroughly disapprove. He/she is extremely excited about his/her newest date, who they claim is the best thing to have ever happened to them. While they believe it's a match made in heaven, you believe it's the ultimate highway to hell. You'd obviously like to help your best friend, but you'd also like to communicate in a manner that doesn't sour things between the two of you. How do you handle the situation?

People with a high emotional quotient will start by objectively evaluating why they dislike their best friend's romantic interest. Are you plain jealous? Does their romantic relationship pose a threat to your relationship with your friend? Does their date remind you of someone whom you have had a terrible experience with? Are you brining your own experiences while evaluating their relationship?

If it is none of this and you are truly convinced that the person is just not good for your friend, you will pose more neutral questions to your friend, which will allow him/her to reflect on the answers on their own rather than go through the agony of hearing their best friend rip apart their romantic interest. If you are emotionally intelligent, you will have a few questions ready to help your friend gather the answers on their own to conclude that the journey with this person may not be as smooth as they are imagining. The idea is to help them realize things on their own without judging, criticizing and making hateful accusations. Also, as someone possessing high emotional intelligence, you must be prepared for being proved wrong.

Let us take another scenario. You have a colleague who you otherwise share a great equation with. She/he is warm, affable and pitches in whenever you require help. However, the problem here is their plainly annoying and overpowering signature perfume. The colleague's sensory receptors seem to be absent and he/she absolutely overdoes the perfume, so much that the suffocating smell makes you sick. You want to voice your objections, yet are wary of offending them because they are genuinely nice. What do you do to make the situation less awkward?

If you are an emotionally intelligent person, you will refrain from offending the other person by being too forthright and assign the blame to your allergies in a more non-confronting and less hurtful manner. Rather than blaming him/her for their tacky fragrance choices that want to make you throw up, you diplomatically assign the onus of blame on your allergies and sensitivities. "I really wish I didn't have such a fine tuned sensory perception." See what we did there? Instead of accusing the other person, you communicated your own allergy or the fact that you and not they are to be blamed for the overpowering smell.

In his bestselling book, "Emotional Intelligence – Why It Can Matter More Than IQ", researcher psychologist Daniel Goleman mentions five crucial elements that define the concept of emotional intelligence.

Self Awareness – People with high emotional intelligence are generally more self aware. They possess a solid understanding of their emotions, the impact of others behavior on their emotions and how their own behavior can affect others. They understand their emotions well enough to not let it rule them. This self awareness makes them more confident, self assured and in control. They rely on their intuition and don't allow emotions to get the better of them.

Self aware people are able to objectively analyze themselves. They are well aware of their strengths and weakness, and use them effectively to achieve the desired results in their personal and professional life. They know what aspects of themselves they need to work on. They seldom live in denial mode. Self awareness is one of the most important aspects of emotional intelligence.

There are several ways to practice self awareness such as meditation, journaling and reflection. For instance, take common stressful scenarios you cope with at work each day such as a team member failing to complete a project on time or being inundated with mails or preparing for an important last minute presentation. What are the emotions these situations elicit in you? Write down your feelings when you are in a more objective mind frame. Include personal stress inducing scenarios too such as being betrayed by a loved one or a breakdown in communication patterns. When you write objectively, it gives you a good insight of your deepest emotions.

Self Regulation – Self regulation is a person's ability to manage or control his/her emotions. Self regulators of feelings and emotions do not allow their emotions to sway them into hasty actions or words. They are seldom angry, impulsive or jealous. Their decisions are well thought out. These are the folks that actually think before acting. People with high emotional self regulation are thoughtful, secure, honest and self-assured. They act with integrity and have little trouble saying no to people where required.

Motivation – People with a high emotional quotient are always raring to go. They are firmly fixated on their goals and motivated to fulfill them. They seldom seek immediate gratification and are willing to give up short term pleasures for long term rewards. Emotionally intelligent people are more solution oriented, productive, challenge embracing and generally efficient in things they take on. Since they operate with a more positive and possibilities mind frame, they are able to stay motivated and chase their goals to fruition.

Empathy – Empathy is the crux of emotional intelligence. It is the ability to recognize and feel the emotions of others from their viewpoint. People with a high empathy quotient are brilliant at identifying others feelings and emotions, even when they aren't very conspicuous. People with high empathy excel at relationship management, listening, and relating to the troubles of others. This makes them wonderful negotiators and leaders. They rarely judge people quickly and their lives are open books.

Social Skills – People with high social skills are effortless to deal with, which is another vital sign of emotional intelligence. They possess powerful social skills and are generally team players. Instead of obsessing over their own success, they believe in helping everyone around them shine and grow. They are very competent when it comes to managing disputes, communicating with people and building lasting relationships. Unlike folks with low emotional intelligence they do not believe in pulling down others to grow or rise in life.

Emotionally intelligent people focus on creating a win-win situation for everyone involved. They are master motivators and communicators. With their knack for handling people, these guys are the most sought after conflict resolvers and negotiators. Little wonder then than emotional intelligence is one of the most preferred attribute at the senior management level.

Social is skills is tantamount for success in every sphere of personal and professional life. In today's well-connected world, people have quick access to technical information. This is exactly why people's skills is even more crucial than technical skills. There is a greater need to be able to negotiate, identify and empathize with people in a worldwide economy. Businesses need people who can wield influence and use effective persuasion techniques by recognizing other's emotions. There is a need to communicate more clearly, and inspiring groups of people.

Organizations need competent change catalysts that can initiate or manage change efficiently. A social skill also involves conflict management, including negotiation skills and resolving differences. Collaboration, teamwork, cooperation and achieving shared goals become simpler when people possess a high emotional quotient. Pursuing collective objectives and building group synergy is effortless for people with well developed social skills and emotional intelligence.

Emotional Intelligence is a greater awareness of your own feelings, emotions and actions, and how they affect people around you. It is also about valuing others, listening to their needs and being able to empathize/identify with these folks on multiple levels. It is about feeling things from their perspective and reacting in a more appropriate and positive manner.

We all know that one person (or more than one person) in our work or personal life, who is an exceptionally good listener. Irrespective of the situation, they always say the right thing. It's almost like they instinctively know what to say. These people know how to say things to make them less offensive for people. They are caring, empathetic and considerate. Emotional intelligent folks may not necessarily have a solution to all your problems but they possess the ability to leave you feeling more positive and hopeful about the grimmest situation.

By now you've probably figured out that emotional quotient can be one of keys to success, especially in your career and interpersonal relationships. The ability to deal with people's emotions and building relationships is the essence of being a leader. Sharpening your emotional quotient can be a great way to bring out your leadership skills. The best part of emotional intelligence is that it can be developed. Even if you don't possess a very high emotional quotient, there's no reason for you to not work on it consciously and sharpen it.

While some people have an inherent gift of harnessing their emotions and weaving them seamlessly into areas such as problem solving, others keenly work on their EQ to forge more rewarding interpersonal and work relationships. They consciously develop a knack of managing and regulating their own emotions, while sharpening their ability to react to other people's emotions.

Little Cynthia watches her mommy finish a call. "Mommy, what makes you cry?" she inquires. "I am alright Cynthia, I will be ok." Cynthia runs to her room and comes back seconds later. "When I feel sad, I hold Candy in my arms", she said, handing her mother her favorite teddy bear. Cynthia knows her mother's sadness but doesn't believe in crippling her even further.

This is how emotional intelligence works. You understand a person's emotions and you don't make it more devastating for them. There is an attempt to comfort them by sharing the best you can. You don't have to judge, sermonize or lecture people. All they need is to feel secure, safe and comforted.

These guys are pros at managing their feelings. They aren't easily offended or angered even in the most stress inducing circumstances. They look at challenging situations more calmly and are more solution oriented. Emotionally intelligent folks are highly tuned in to their intuition for making important decisions. They have the ability to evaluate themselves more objectively by handling criticism rather well and knowing their areas of improvement.

When we develop the gift of better managing people's emotions and empathizing with their unique perspective, conflict resolution becomes easier. You become a better leader, negotiator, mentor, friend and other roles by being aware of the most compelling needs and desires of others. When you know the fundamental emotions that drive, it is easy to manage to manage your behavior to create a win-win situation. It becomes simpler to give people exactly what they are looking for if you are able to intuitively perceive their needs.

Jason was a highly accomplished and successful manager well-known for his knack of handling challenging organization issues and getting impressive results. He assessed situations accurately, made solid decisions, and took ownership of company projects. Jason swiftly rose from the role of a divisional manager to a senior management position within the firm.

He continued to lobby for senior organizational leadership positions and proactively sought an increase in his functional responsibilities by taking on more challenging problems. He rose to the senior management rank quickly.

Jason was confident, and others believed he would inevitably reach the echelons of management success. He did not end up in the senior executive suite. In fact, his career went downhill and the management had to look for substitutes to reassign his responsibilities. What do you think went wrong with this rather promising manager? Why did his journey to the top go off the course?

This is the story of most senior managers. While they are able to manage people at the junior management level, micromanaging managers and delegating independent authority at the senior level becomes tough. Jason was capable of getting through his behavior at the lower management level. However, once the organization became too large for his control, it was impossible to manage an efficient working relationship with senior managers.

Jason's inability to delegate authority and obsession for micromanagement were indicators of a much larger issue – he simply lacked emotional intelligence. This illustration explains why senior managers need huge reserves of emotional intelligence. Jason struggled with understanding and managing his emotions. This self awareness deficit translated into being unable to comprehend and manage other's emotions.

Jason's greatest handicap was his insecurity and fear. He feared about losing control over his organizational domain if he ceased to micromanage each aspect. His fear of being replaced if his team did their jobs only too well or being unable to control his managers if he gave them complete authority led to his dwindling fortunes. Jason became a victim of his own inability to manage his and the team's emotions.

When negative emotions are unmanageable, organizations are prone to produce disastrous results. It can result in stunted productivity, strained relationships, unmet business objectives and higher absenteeism.

According to a study, surgeons involved in malpractice suits had lesser chances of being sued if they spent an extra 3 minutes doing the following – making orienting statements, using reassuring words and communicating empathy.

Let's do a short self evaluation here to gauge your Emotional Quotient.

1 Are you able to identify your own emotions?

2 Do you quickly register the emotions of other people or are able to understand how they are feeling?

3 Can you point out exactly what triggers emotions within you?

4 Can you control or organize your emotional informational?

5 Are you willing to admit to and learn from mistakes easily?

6 Are you able to control your emotions?

7 Can you listen more than you talk or at least as equivalent to how much you talk?

8 Can you handle criticism positively?

9 Are you calm and composed under the most intense pressure situations?

These questions will help you reflect where you stand in the emotional quotient meter. However, fret not if you do not consider yourself an emotional intelligence superstar. There are tons of ways to boost your EQ.

Chapter 2: Difference between Intelligence Quotient and Emotional Quotient

How does emotional quotient differ from intelligence quotient? The simple answer is- they measure different forms of intelligence. Your technical acumen or technical skills is a direct result of a high intelligence quotient. You've mastered your skills well, which is a reflection of well-developed cognitive abilities. However, is intelligent quotient enough to determine your success when it comes to dealing with people (unless you are cooped up on a remote island all yourself, you have to deal with people)?

While intelligence quotient measures your technical expertise, emotional quotient evaluates your ability to manage your and other people's emotions in your work and personal life. You know where every employee stands when it comes to technical prowess but do you really understand their thoughts, actions and feelings to be able to better manage your and their behavior in sync with these emotions. When we gain insights into the underlying emotional patterns of people, it becomes easier to relate to them and channelize more productive behavior. This is a fundamental difference between intelligence quotient and emotional quotient.

Ever wondered why some of the cleverest people hit a blank in their professional lives and just can't seem to climb the corporate ladder, while the less knowledgeable and inexperienced folks smoothly sail their way to professional success? We all know of people who don't exactly possess the slickest technical skills yet surprisingly manage to reach top management positions. What is it that sets them apart from their more technically competent peers? Emotional intelligence is the key. It is their ability to recognize and control their and other's emotions to build more productive relationships that helps them score.

A person's intelligence quotient demonstrates their core technical competencies, cognitive development and unusual abilities, their emotional intelligence determines their ability to identify emotions and deal with others. Your emotional quotient determines how you will deal with stress, difficult people, bullying, high pressure work situations, conflict within the team, and differences in relationships.

Intelligence is an indicator of your cognitive prowess such as logical thinking, analytical reasoning, memorizing information, solving problems, verbal abilities, creative thinking and much more. Emotional intelligence is controlling your and other's emotions for creating optimally positive circumstances. Starkly different from your ability to comprehend words and numbers, emotional quotient helps you develop healthy interpersonal relationships in your personal and work life.

Emotional intelligence can include stress management, intuition, emotional flexibility, empathy, honestly and more. Emotional quotient highlights your and others emotions with respect to changing circumstances and people, while intelligence quotient is all about cognitive abilities.

While intelligence quotient can determine your success during your academic stint, emotional quotient is vital for all round success in life. You may excel as a student if you possess a high intelligence quotient. However to attain overall success in life, you need a high emotional quotient.

Research has indicated that there are five fundamental skills that distinguish the star performers from low performers. These skills are empathy, self-awareness, assertiveness, problem solving and happiness. Potential recruits who score high on these five attributes are 2.7 times likelier to succeed than folks who bag low scores.

So, why is emotional quotient so closely associated with a person's chances of becoming successful in life? The answer is – awareness of emotions and ability to express themselves confidently. Emotionally intelligent people are experts in gauging people's emotions and altering their pitches/presentations accordingly. Little wonder then that emotionally intelligence is so vital for people in sales, customer service, counseling and other industries.

For instance, a study closely followed the recruitment of sales personnel for cosmetic giant L'Oreal based on their emotional skills. It was observed that these emotionally competent sales people outdid other salespersons by a whopping $91,370 to amass a net revenue growth of $ 2,558, 360. In another research, a national insurance firm discovered that salespersons who were low on emotional skills like initiative, confidence and empathy sold far less policies (average premium of $54,000) that agents who scored high on emotional skills (average premium of $114,000). You get the picture, right? When you show high emotional competencies by being proactive, self confident and empathetic, you are able to connect to potential buyers and help them buy rather than simply sell.

In the workplace, intelligence quotient helps for analyzing, connecting the dots and undertaking research and development. Emotional intelligence is about forging a strong team spirit, leadership, building successful professional relationships, collaboration, service and initiative. Emotional quotient can be gained and enhanced as opposed to intelligence quotient, which is a more inborn and hereditary characteristic.

The goal for businesses isn't to simply hire people who are intellectually competent, but lack emotional or people skills. Today's competitive and social interactions dominated world demands workers who are smart (that's a given), and endowed with more thoughtfulness. The ideal candidate is a combination of emotional intelligence and general intelligence. Since all candidates applying for a position possess more or less the same technical competence, emotional intelligence often becomes a clinching factor when it comes to selecting people for important roles.

Standford-Binet, Woodcock-Johnson Tests of Cognitive abilities and Wechsler are some popular intelligence quotient tests, while Mayer-Salovey-Caruso Test and Daniel Goleman model score test are popular emotional intelligence assessment tests. An Intelligence Quotient test generally involves a collection of standardized questions where participants are assigned precise scores based on their answers. These scores are evaluated with respect to average scores within the age group to establish a person's intellectual capabilities.

Emotional quotient tests, on the other hand, are more challenging to administer because feelings and emotional skills are tougher to depict numerically. While intelligence quotient questions have a definite answer for every question, emotional quotient tests tend to be more subjective and require greater evaluation effort. Unlike IQ tests, there aren't any right or wrong answers. Respondents may not answer questions honestly simply to rank high or may adjust their responses according to what they are currently experiencing, which makes these results more skewed. There may be a tendency on part of the participant to say exactly what the evaluators want to hear rather than responding truthfully.

People possessing a high intelligence quotient are excellent at conducting tasks. They are quick absorbers of new skills and information. However, if they have a low emotional quotient, they tend to overlook their and other's feelings. For instance, when something doesn't turn out according to the way they wanted, these folks tend to lose their temper and lash out at people. While someone who is high on emotional intelligence will learn to control their emotions and get along with people around them. They are extremely effective when it comes to working as a team or working in a leadership role.

The concept of emotional intelligence has gained such a strong momentum that it has impacted a large a large number of areas including the corporate world. Several top organizations have now made emotional intelligence tests mandatory as part of the hiring process, along with intelligence quotient.

In personal relationships, 90 percent of the issues arise due to lack of emotional intelligence. Everything revolves around empathy, self awareness, awareness of the other person's emotions, understanding, communication patterns and the likes, which are all components of emotional intelligence.

Emotional quotient is not the antithesis of intelligence quotient. They aren't mutually exclusive. Some folks possess both in huge quantities, while others possess neither. Psychologists are keener to explore how the two attributes balance each other. For instance, how your ability to deal with stress impacts your ability to focus or learn new information.

Chapter 3: Benefits of Emotional Intelligence

As discussed earlier, emotional intelligence is our ability to manage our and other's emotions by discriminating among these feelings, and using the information to guide our words, thoughts and actions. To cut a long story short, emotional intelligence is an aggregation of your mental and emotional skills. Emotionally intelligent people enjoy a multitude of benefits in all spheres of life including relationships, career and social life. Here are some ways in which your life can be impacted or benefited if you consciously focus on developing high emotional intelligence.

Stellar Productivity

Emotional intelligence has a high correlation with an individual's work performance. Research has revealed that emotional intelligence is twice as crucial as technical/cognitive abilities even among professions such as engineering. Emotionally intelligent managers, supervisors and leaders are way more effective in managing teams, motivating people and negotiating.

They create a more positive atmosphere with happier workers, who are an asset to any organization. Happier workers translate into higher morale, low absenteeism, reduced attrition rate and higher productivity. This leads to happier customers, more sales and higher profits. Thus emotional intelligence is an invaluable trait when it comes to success at the workplace. Whilst everyone within an organization possesses more or less the same technical competency and educational qualifications, only a few rise up the corporate ladder because of their ability to manage people and their emotions.

An emotionally intelligent leader who understands the true value of identifying and managing emotions can empower his/her subordinates with these skills on a daily basis. Discipline or self regulation is essential when it comes to keeping your emotions in check, avoiding panic, remaining calm and being an asset to the team. Emotionally intelligent folks have little trouble in recognizing and managing potentially destructive emotions that can create stress and lower productivity. The approach is calmer, more confident and efficient. Rather than experiencing a more touchy view, these folks depend on their ability to possess a more realistic view of themselves and others.

Coping With Life Challenges

Don't you sometimes look at some people and wonder how they are able to stay afloat through the most challenging situations and emerge even more successful than before? Chances are, these guys score high on emotional intelligence. Emotionally intelligent folks have the ability to calm their body and mind to view things from a clearer and more objective perspective. Their acts are more mindful and less panic struck.

Greater calmness, objectivity and clarity award you more resilience where life's challenges are concerned. Think about the kungfu fighter who can take on the most powerful opponents by constantly working on martial arts skills. Emotional intelligence equips you with those skills to take on the toughest challenges life throws at you with resilience.

Greater Compassion in Personal and Work Life

One of the best benefits of high emotional intelligence is your ability to demonstrate more compassion for others both in the personal and professional sphere. This compassion allows them to connect with people at much deeper levels to forge meaningful relationships. Compassion can be manifested in several ways, including helping someone dealing with a personal issue by taking on their responsibilities or making small everyday decisions for the comfort/convenience of your employees.

Compassion helps you meaningfully connect with people both in your personal and professional life. You are able to reach out to people efficiently, forge more mutually fulfilling relationships and create an atmosphere of harmony and productivity. Emotional intelligence awards you greater compassion in dealing with people in various personal professional and social scenarios.

Boosted Leadership Skills

Emotionally intelligent folks possess a highly evolved ability in recognizing and understanding factors that drive others, which makes them amazing leaders. They are able to make the most of this invaluable information to strengthen their loyalty and forge stronger relationships with people. A competent leader is intuitively tuned in to the most compelling aspirations and desires of his followers. He knows the "hot buttons" of his employees and exactly how to channelize these "hot buttons" to increase overall productivity and positivity within the work environment.

Emotionally intelligent leaders know how to channelize this information for extracting better performance/productivity from people and keeping them happy. People with a high emotional quotient excel at recognizing the strengths and weaknesses of people and harnessing an individual's virtues for benefiting the team.

High emotional intelligence creates better leaders who are able to inspire greater faith and loyalty by using their team's or follower's or emotional range. They are more aware of their emotions, which allow emotionally intelligent folks to create a harmonious environment. Practicing emotional intelligence makes you a better leader.

Did you know that 67% of all competencies said to be fundamental for high performance in the professional sphere is emotional intelligence? Take the example of the world's most successful CEOs. Amazon's Jeff Bezos passionately talks about getting right into the hearts of his customers in a 2009 YouTube video while announcing the company's Zappos acquisition. When Howard Schultz of Starbucks was a child, his father lost a health insurance claim. This turned him into one of the most empathetic CEOs, who is well known showing his employees thoughtfulness by offering generous healthcare rewards. Little wonder then that these folks are as successful as they are. They understand the emotional pulse of their employees and customers to keep them emotionally gratified.

Emotional intelligence helps in building emotional maturity, boosting social intelligence, preventing relationship problems, enhancing interpersonal communication, helping control emotions, dealing with stress, influencing leadership, helping authorities make sound business change decisions, supporting staff and controlling resistance to change.

Lower Chances of Addiction and Other Emotional Disorders

Addictions are generally a direct result of our inability to cope with emotions. People who struggle to come to terms with their emotions use addiction as a mechanism to avoid the more underlying and deeper prevailing issues. When you fail to recognize and manage negative emotions, there develops an unfortunate pattern of dependency on external factors such as food, nicotine, substance, alcohol, porn and the likes.

Addiction is just a means to escape from emotions you aren't willing to deal with.

Emotionally intelligent folks are lesser prone to addiction because of their awareness of their emotions and the ability to manage these emotions. They have a solid understanding of their feelings, and do not struggle to deal with it. Since emotional intelligence makes you happier, more confident and balanced, there is a lesser propensity for dependence on destructive coping mechanisms. They adapt more easily to challenges and changing scenarios in life. Emotionally intelligent people are competent in resolving differences and coming up with more positive solutions. Since they display such a high understanding of their and other's emotions, it becomes easier for them to deal with conflicts.

Emotionally healthy people are less prone to be victims of drug abuse or binge eating disorders, which predominantly originate from much deeper psychological issues.

Boosted Employee Morale and Lower Attrition

Morale may be an intangible concept in the corporate world but its effects are highly measureable. You may not realize the value of a high morale when it's there, but you will definitely know when it's missing. Think about the lateness, early departures, attrition, sick leaves your company suffers from. When leaders take the time to build emotional intelligence and connect with their team members, it reflects in the employee morale.

Emotionally intelligent leaders who build stronger emotional ties with subordinates witness improvement in the team's morale, lower measureable absenteeism, a higher team spirit and a greater desire to contribute to an organization's success. The emotional intelligence skill building cost can be minimal. However, the return on investment can be extremely high.

Let's get real here and call a spade a spade. Employees do not really quit roles, they quit senior managers. It is about escaping people and not positions. Emotionally intelligent leaders, who recognize emotional triggers, quickly pick up emotional clues of their team members and "customize" their approach to each member's unique emotional make-up and motivation will experience greater success in retaining employees. This should not be mistaken with not doing justice to one's own voice or feelings. It simply means, presenting an accurate emotional response towards each team member to treat them with greater compassion, respect and empathy.

The problem with most managers who do not understand the concept of emotional intelligence is that they use a one size fits all approach for dealing with all employees, without understanding the emotional framework, motivators and goals of individual team members. This one size fits all approach does not produce flattering results because personalities vary. Some people are more intrinsically motivated, while others thrive on extrinsic motivation. Some folks are quick to reveal their emotions; others aren't very comfortable sharing their feelings. Once you understand the emotional make-up of people, it becomes easy to deal with them more efficiently.

Fine Communication Skills

People with a well developed emotional quotient are more efficient when it comes to expressing themselves. They possess the ability to listen attentively to other people's verbal clues, while also tuning in to their non verbal communication. They know exactly what to say to channelize people's strengths. They use the right words and non verbal signals to help people feel at ease. There is little scope for misunderstanding whilst communicating with a person who has high emotional intelligence.

Emotionally intelligent people are well aware about the most compelling emotional triggers of the people around them. They know exactly how to inspire people to act. People who are able to communicate by emotionally connecting with are far more effective than technically competent folks who fail to demonstrate empathy while communicating with people. Emotional intelligence awards you better response skills.

Chapter 4: Proven Tips to Boost Your Emotional Intelligence

After gaining a thorough understanding of emotional intelligence and its benefits, the million dollar question is – is it really possible to improve one's emotional intelligence or emotional quotient? Is it possible from struggling to cope with your and other's emotions to being a rockstar at understanding emotions?

With all its advantages, who wouldn't want high emotional intelligence? Who wouldn't want greater professional success, business potential, leadership skills, relationship gratification, humor, good healthy, positivity and happiness around them? Think about an antidote that beats stress, helps you form rewarding relationships with people and much more.

Take any coaching intervention program, and it will generally highlight some aspect of emotional intelligence in the name of interpersonal skills or social/soft skills. The most compelling reason for this is that, while intelligence quotient is tough to change, emotional quotient can be acquired with training and consistent practice. So, the good news is that even if you do not consider yourself very emotionally evolved, there is plenty of scope to boost your emotional quotient with practice, training and conscious effort.

 The best part about enhancing your emotional intelligence is that it can be practiced in your everyday life. For instance, if you are short tempered, start by showing greater empathy or being a more considerate listener.

Emotional Quotient Is Not Rigid

Though our capacity to recognize and handle our and other's emotions is largely determined by childhood experiences, heredity and other factors, it isn't rigid. We can alter our ability to comprehend and manage emotions over the long term with the right coaching and dedication. You can change of course, however, the question is do you want to change? Are you willing to put in the effort required to be more emotionally intelligent? Sometimes, while you may successfully be able to manage your external emotions, you may still grapple with emotions you do not manage to display on the outside.

While some folks are naturally positive, calm and social, others can be plain grumpy, egoistic, shy or insecure. However, no trait is unchangeable. If you truly want to change an aspect of your personality, you can. Emotional intelligence naturally increases with age, without any intervention. This is the rationale behind the popular belief that people gain more maturity as they grow older. Overall, yes it is possible to improve your emotional quotient over the long term with intervention, guidance and regular practice.

Emotional Intelligence Be Developed

Our emotional intelligence pathway originates within the brain going right down to the spinal cord. The primary senses are involved here and must go to the brain's front portion before you start thinking logically or rationally about an occurrence. Emotions are generated in our limbic system, which is why our emotional response to an incident occurs before the rational mind gets involved. Emotional intelligence is based on efficient communication patterns between the brain's logical and emotional points.

Have you heard of plasticity? It is a term used by neurologists for describing the brain's ability to keep evolving and changing.

The brain keeps growing newer connections as we acquire new skills. The change is slow, as the brain keeps developing more and more connections to boost its efficiency.

When you use various strategies for boosting emotional intelligence, you are actually letting the microscopic neurons (billions of them) lined between the emotional and logical centers of the brain to branch into smaller arms that touch other cells. This simply means, one cell can form more than 15,000 connections. The chain reaction signifies that it is simpler for the brain to adapt to this new behavior in the long term. Once the brain is trained with the help of emotional intelligence strategies, it becomes a habitual behavior/thought pattern.

Accurate Feedback

One of the most crucial aspects if you want to enhance your emotional quotient through any coaching intervention or self practice program is accurate feedback. People generally do not realize how others perceive them, especially people in senior management positions in organizations.

Though these folks are increasingly motivated, responsible and high on technical skills, they rarely take the time to pause and assess their behavior. In a nutshell, we do not possess a very accurate notion of how nice we come across as. Wishful thinking, misplaced optimism and overconfidence can be factors contributing to this blind spot.

Generally people tend to over evaluate themselves in the niceness department. They believe they are nicer than they actually are. Any effort at increasing your emotional quotient must begin with gaining a thorough understanding your strengths and weaknesses. Use valid and genuine assessment techniques like personality tests or accurate feedback to determine your success with developing a higher emotional quotient.

Some Methods Work More Efficiently Than Others

Some techniques for boosting emotional intelligence such as cognitive behavioral therapy for better psychological flexibility can work better than other methods. Since emotional intelligence is linked to human behavior, it can never be an exact science. The dynamics of human behavior, motivation, communication and feelings will keep changing. You have to identify and evaluate what works for you. While behavioral therapy works wonderfully well for some people, others may find meditation or deep breathing more effective in calming their emotions.

Here are some tried and tested tips for being the ultimate emotional intelligence ninja.

Respond Rather Than React

Reacting is a more unconscious and uncontrolled process that is a result of an emotional trigger. For instance, you snap when someone annoys you or you are already stressed due to another reason.

Responding, on the other hand, is more controlled and something you choose to do. You decide exactly how you behave in the given situation. For example, explaining to someone that you are not feeling too good and that this isn't the best time to interrupt you, and that later you'd be in a much better position to give them a good hearing. You've simply chosen to deal with the situation in a more productive and less impulsive manner by taking control of your emotions.

Evaluate how your actions will impact others before acting. If your behavior will affect others, try and place yourself in their shoes. How are they bound to feel if you say or do something? Would you like to go through the experience yourself? If you have to take a particular action, can you help people in coping with its effects?

Accept Responsibility for Your Feelings and Actions

This can be one of the most challenging yet productive tips for boost your emotional quotient. Your emotions originate from you and therefore you are completely responsible for them.

People around you may be responsible for creating certain situations but it is ultimately you who are in charge of your reaction to those situations. You may not always be able to control how others around you speak or behave. However, the way you react to their words and actions is something you have control over.

If you are hurt by someone and lash out, you are the one responsible for it. Get out of the mindset that "someone makes you do something." No one can make you angry; you are responsible for your anger. No one holds the strings to your emotions. No one makes you do or feel anything. Your reaction is completely your own responsibility. Your feelings can offer you important guidelines about your experience with different people along with your own requirements and preferences. However, your feelings and actions are no one's but your responsibility.

Once you start accepting responsibility for your feelings and behavior, it becomes simpler to manage it for impacting all spheres of your life positively.

If you hurt people, be gracious enough to accept it and apologize. Ignoring the person or not accepting the responsibility for your behavior is not a sign of high emotional intelligence. Your relationships will be much more positive and people will forgive you more easily if you make an honest attempt to set things right rather than live in denial land.

Accepting your mistakes, apologizing and moving on is a sign of high emotional intelligence.

Be Assertive

Emotionally intelligent folks know the importance of setting appropriate boundaries to let people know our stand. You have the right to disagree with people without acting in a disagreeable manner. Learn to say refuse without feeling guilty when you are not up to something or you find people taking advantage of you. Set your priorities and safeguard yourself from stress, harm and duress.

Rather than using "you" followed by the accusation and putting people on the defensive foot, try making them more open to listening to and understanding your point. For instance, instead of saying "you should do this" or "you are xyx", try saying, "I feel really uncomfortable when you expect me to do this over my priorities" or "I strongly believe that I deserve recognition from the organization based on my consistent performance and contributions." See what we did there? We aren't putting people on the defensive by pointing a finger at them and saying, "you did this" or "you are like this." We are being assertive and talking about our feelings without blaming anybody.

Pay Close Attention to Your Behavior

You can only manage your emotions more effectively if you are consciously aware of it. It starts with paying very close attention to your emotions and their impact on your behavior. Emotional awareness is one of the cornerstones of EQ.

Start noticing how you act when you experience specific situations, and how it affects your everyday life. Do these feelings impact your productivity? How about your communication with other people? Do your emotions pose a threat to your overall well-being, including your physical and emotional health? How do you react when you are extremely angry, happy or sad? Once you are consciously aware of your reactions to emotions, you will be able to wield better control over them and channelize them more productively.

Practice Empathy

Empathy is all about trying to understand why someone feels or acts in the way they do by putting yourself in their shoes. It is also being able to communicate this understanding to them more effectively. Empathy can also apply to your emotions and feelings.

Each time you notice yourself experiencing a specific emotion or behavior, try and think why you feel the way you do. You may not be able to figure it out at the onset but pay close attention and you'll start receiving various answers that you didn't notice earlier.

When someone is experiencing a rather strong feeling, ask yourself how you would feel in a similar scenario. Always be interested in what people say to respond in a more sensitive manner. It is always a good practice to ask questions and summarize what people say so you are clear, and people know you are actively listening to them.

When you put yourself in the other person's shoe, you reduce reactivity. For instance, if your child is resisting something you are telling him/her, try thinking it isn't easy for them to deal with peer pressure and academics. Think for a moment how it must be to be a young kid in the current competitive age.

 If your manager is being demanding and difficult, think about the pressure of performance expectation they are dealing with at the hands of senior management. When you start thinking more objectively by considering where the other person is coming from, understanding and conflict resolution become much simpler.

Managing other's emotions requires maturity, skill and tact. It starts by being aware of exactly where you want the person to go? Do you want to lead them to feeling happier, calmer, more aware, secure, vigilant or cautious, for instance? Once you realize how they are feeling and how to lead them there, you will know what to say and do.

We tend to forget how particular experiences feel; even we've lived through it ourselves. You can only imagine how much perspective limiting it becomes if we've not experienced what the other person is going through. What is the best way to bridge this gap? The nucleus of empathy lies in understanding the "why" among other things. Why does this person feel the way they do? What are they dealing with that I fail to see? Why do I experience different feelings than them? Explore your "whys" and you will be well on your way to better understanding the feelings of others.

Being kind, considerate and helpful is one of the best ways of practicing emotional intelligence.

Avoid Labeling Your Emotions

All your emotions are valid, including the not so positive ones. Avoid assigning labels and judging your emotions. When you judge your feelings, you inhibit your ability to experience them. When you cannot fully express or experience something, you prevent yourself from using these emotions more positively.

Each emotion you experience is a vital piece of information closely linked with what is happening around you and how it affects you. Without information about your emotions, you'd be left clueless about how to react to your emotions and manage them more effectively.

Connect negative feelings to events but avoid judging them to gain a better understanding. For instance, if you feel envious, try and figure out what the emotions is conveying to you about the situation. Learn to experience positive emotions so you recognize each opportunity to feel them to the fullest.

Practice Being More Light Hearted

When you are more light hearted and optimistic, it is simpler to capture the goodness of everyday situations and objects. Positivity results in greater emotional happiness and increased opportunities. People are forever looking to be around optimistic folks who come up with positive connections and possibilities. When you become more negative, you only concentrate on what can go awry rather than building strong resistance.

People with a more evolved emotional quotient know how to utilize wit and humor to make everyone feel happier, positive and safer. They know the art of using laugher to tide over tough times.

Use Your Mental Pause Button

Use your mental pause button each time you find yourself on the verge of speaking or acting. Take a moment, breathe deeply and think before you respond. Whenever you feel tempted to type an elaborate mail in rage, stop and think if it is going to help resolve the issue or only make it worse. Each time you feel like screaming at someone or making a combustible comment on the social media, apply the pause button.

When you consciously work on pausing before you speak or act, you get into the habit of thinking before acting or speaking in a manner that can worsen any situation. You learn to manage, control and tackle your emotions to handle any situation in a more constructive manner. When you learn to use this technique, you realize that the button to your feelings and emotions is in your hands.

When you sense a challenge in controlling impulses, deal with it by quickly diverting your attention. Distract your thoughts by counting or concentrating on a pre-planned diversion thought. Your mind can be trained to shift thoughts or conversations fast.

Practice Active Listening

During arguments or disagreements we often listen not to understand but to react and respond. When the other person is speaking, we are almost mentally constructing out own arguments to answer back or give back to them. This leads to even more conflict.

Dealing with conflict becomes more effective when you tackle issues in an assertive yet respective manner, without being defensive. When you listen empathetically, your own thoughts and emotions are taken into account. Listening actively and empathetically can help you shed toxic feelings building up in you.

Be assertive by all means, but also practice active listening to find that one point that can lead to resolution. Problem solution only happens when you understand where the other person is coming from and what they want. You can find a middle ground only when you tune in to the words, feelings and emotions of the other person, not just to give a fitting reply but also to resolve the issue. Listening is all about putting the other person's words, thoughts and feelings first.

Your opinion about people or events may not change. However, the time spent listening to the other person may just calm you and help you come up with a more positive or constructive response. It may help you see things from a different perspective and analyze the situation more objectively.

Be Open to Feedback

Boost your emotional intelligence by being more receptive to feedback. While you may disagree with the criticism/feedback, sometimes being open to other's views can help you identify behavior patterns that may be having an effect that you didn't intend. Healthy feedback can guard you from blind spots and adjust your behavior.

The more you exist in denial mode about destructive behavior, the more challenging it may be for you to develop a high emotional quotient. Acceptance and awareness is the key to increasing your emotional intelligence.

Practice Deep Breathing

Strong emotions impact us physically too. When we are stressed or anxious, our bodies respond in a more evolutionary instinctive manner like we're face to face with a nature based threat. The physical reactions include constricted blood vessels, shallow breathing and speedier heart rate.

When we learn to consciously manage our body's reaction to anxiety, the emotional attribute is lowered. Each time you feel nervous or tense, practice slow and deep breathing. Concentrate on the flow of the breath and the abdominal cavity. You will invariably feel better and calmer once you relax and create more space in your mind.

Mindfulness or mindful breathing is another way to achieve stillness of the mind by completely immersing yourself in the present non-judgmentally. When you get into the habit of identifying your thoughts and emotions with judgment, you boost your awareness and gain greater clarity rather than operating from a judgmental and assumption laden point of view. Mindfulness reduces your chances of being overtaken by negative or destructive emotions.

Decrease Negative Personalization

When we feel negatively impacted by someone's behavior, do not rush into a conclusion. Tempting as it is to ascribe a negative reason for their behavior, try to gather a more holistic perspective of the circumstances before reacting. For instance, it is easy to think a friend isn't returning your call or message because he/she wants to avoid you.

However, they may also be busy or ill or in a dire situation. When we avoid ascribing negative reasons or personalizing people's behavior, we view them more objectively and with less hateful/judgmental emotions. The ability to overcome negative personalization of people's behavior is critical for boosting your emotional quotient.

Develop Flexibility

Sometimes we get stuck in our own monotonous traps and become rigid and inflexible, which may impair our emotional intelligence. People with a highly developed emotional quotient know when to adapt and keep pace with newer techniques rather than getting stuck in an increasingly unproductive cycle. They know when how to adapt and manage their emotions according to the situation. Emotionally intelligent folks know when to adapt and shift perceptions.

Those who possess a highly developed emotional quotient are always open to newer experiences, challenging opportunities and a variety of adventures. Be open to change and shed the uneasiness and inhibitions attached with change.

Learn to decipher the consequences of your words and behavior. Emotionally intelligent folks pick their battles very selectively. They realize that peace and relationships are more valuable than being right.

When you learn to evaluate the consequences of your words and actions and demonstrate more flexibility and adaptability in your actions/words, you display high emotional intelligence. This isn't to be mistaken with letting people walk all over you. By all means, be assertive. However, know that it's not about being right or winning arguments all the time. Emotional intelligence is being perspective enough to realize what is worth fighting for and what is worth giving up.

Read Body Language

Try to gauge people's innermost emotions by tuning in to their body language. Pick up clues about their emotional health by observing their body language. Sometimes people say something while their expressions and gestures convey the opposite or a deeper truth they aren't comfortable revealing. When you practice being more mindful of their body language, you tap into their true emotional fabric to adapt you responses and reactions. Sometimes people resort to less conspicuous ways for communicating their emotions.

For instance, a person may try saying something reassuring but the high tone of their voice may defeat those words and indicate high stress. These are small yet powerful indicators of people's behavior patterns and reading them correctly will give you the power to unlock other's emotional framework.

Be Emotionally Honest

Be emotionally honest and transparent. You are not communicating genuinely if you shut yourself off from expressing emotions. If you say you are alright with a sorrowful face, you are being dishonest in your communication. When you practice being more real about emotions, it is easier for people to read it. It is always great to be able to be yourself and share your real feelings. It helps people know your feelings and understand where you are coming from. They trust you more, which sets the base for more rewarding relationships.

By all means manage your emotions so as to avoid hurting others but misleading others about your emotions or denying real deeper emotions is not a sign of high emotional intelligence.

Be Positive and Happy

How would you rate your happiness quotient on a scale of 1 to 10? Emotional intelligence originates from being happy and vice versa. They aren't simply happy because good things are happening to them but because they are great at managing and taking control of their own happiness.

Happiness originates from within. A person who is capable of managing his emotions efficiently wakes up joyfully each morning. These people encounter challenges too, just like everyone else. However, they do not let these issues dampen their zest for positivity. Develop greater emotional intelligence by keeping your mind clear, avoid getting caught in destructive self-pity and take charge of your happiness. Emotional intelligence comes with being more positive and solution oriented.

Happy people gain more appreciation and following from people to help them tide over tough times. They spread more happiness, live longer and come up with constructive solution. It is a misconception that happiness is a result of material possessions. Genuinely happy people are those who can manage their emotions well, spread happiness, and most importantly those who focus on giving rather than receiving. Emotionally intelligent people know that it costs zilch to be happy and yet the returns are invaluable.

Stop Complaining

One of the first steps towards boosting your emotional intelligence is to stop complaining. Shed the victim syndrome and know that the solution to your problem is well within your grasp. Emotionally intelligent people rarely blame others or their circumstances for the challenges in their life. Instead, they search for matured ways to dissolve a relationship or talk to people who've wronged them in private. They also have a steady stream of effective coping mechanisms such as yoga, meditation, nature trips or simply venting their feelings by writing.

Listen to Physical Clues

Some of the best indicators of our emotional condition are the physical signals our body gives us. You can develop a greater awareness of your emotions simply by tuning in to your physical sensations. You may feel a knot in your tummy while commuting to work, which can be a sign of high stress.

Similarly, when you are with someone you've recently started dating, and experience a too strong to ignore flutter in your heart, it could be an indication of having found the person who'd like to spend the rest of your life with. Our body is constantly trying to communicate emotions we may not be aware of through physical sensations. Listening to these feelings and emotions signaled by the body helps process our emotions and reactions more efficiently.

Tap Into Your Subconscious Mind

How can you gain a greater awareness of your subconscious emotions or feelings? Apart from deep breathing and mindfulness, let your thoughts wander freely and evaluate where they go. Pay close attention to your dreams. Are there any recurring symbols that can be closely connected with the current events in your life?

Keep a journal and pen next to your bed and write down the details you can recall about your most compelling dreams as soon as you are up. Analyze the emotions and patterns of these dreams, their symbolic references and the message they are trying to communicate. When you gain a thorough understanding of the emotions that dominate your subconscious mind, it becomes simpler to train your subconscious mind to guide your actions.

Sometimes, our conscious minds are unable to come with solutions we are faced with, which is why the phrase "sleep over it" originated. Our subconscious mind's functionality is at its peak when we are asleep. Ever wondered why many a times the solution to our problems strikes us when we are asleep? Or we wake up with a totally different perspective or solution much to our surprise? Our subconscious mind is ticking overtime when our conscious mind is resting. By tuning into our subconscious mind, we are tapping into our inner most emotional reserve to uncover our deepest feelings.

Resolve Conflicts Like a Boss

One of the best tips for developing high emotional quotient is mastering conflict management skills. Conflict resolution actually puts your emotional intelligence to practical use. Resolving differences and conflicts involves many aspects including identifying feelings, clear expression of thoughts, active listening, staying calm and coming up with a solution that diffuses the situation rather than escalating it. When we struggle to understand and control our feeling, we experience a sense of irritation, depression and erratic behavior patterns. Conflicts only get magnified, making it all the more stressful for to deal with. Once you recognize yours and other's emotions, and learn to manage them, you enjoy a happier and more balanced life.

Conclusion

Thank you for downloading this book.

I hope the book was able to help you to understand the powerful concept of emotional intelligence and how you can use it in your everyday life to enjoy more rewarding personal and professional relationships.

There are lots of real life examples, actionable tips and practical pointers on how you can go about boosting your emotional quotient right away.

The next step is to simply take action and follow the proven techniques mentioned in the book.

Here's to your rewarding, enriching and emotionally healthy relationships!

Emotional Intelligence Mastery

How to Master Your Emotions, Improve Your EQ, and Massively Improve Your Relationships

© Copyright 2017 by Ryan James - All rights reserved.

The following Book is reproduced below with the goal of providing information that is as accurate and as reliable as possible. Regardless, purchasing this Book can be seen as consent to the fact that both the publisher and the author of this book are in no way experts on the topics discussed within, and that any recommendations or suggestions made herein are for entertainment purposes only. Professionals should be consulted as needed before undertaking any of the action endorsed herein.

This declaration is deemed fair and valid by both the American Bar Association and the Committee of Publishers Association and is legally binding throughout the United States.

Furthermore, the transmission, duplication or reproduction of any of the following work, including precise information, will be considered an illegal act, irrespective whether it is done electronically or in print. The legality extends to creating a secondary or tertiary copy of the work or a recorded copy and is only allowed with express written consent of the Publisher. All additional rights are reserved.

The information in the following pages is broadly considered to be a truthful and accurate account of facts, and as such any inattention, use or misuse of the information in question by the reader will render any resulting actions solely under their purview. There are no scenarios in which the publisher or the original author of this work can be in any fashion deemed liable for any hardship or damages that may befall them after undertaking information described herein.

Additionally, the information found on the following pages is intended for informational purposes only and should thus be considered, universal. As befitting its nature, the information presented is without assurance regarding its continued validity or interim quality. Trademarks that mentioned are done without written consent and can in no way be considered an endorsement from the trademark holder.

Introduction

Congratulations on the purchase of this book, *Emotional Intelligence Mastery: How to Master Your Emotions, Improve Your EQ, and Massively Improve Your Relationships*. This book is written as a sequel to the book *Emotional Intelligence: The definitive guide to understanding your emotions, how to improve your EQ and your relationships*. This book is for those who have learned what Emotional Intelligence (EQ) is and how it effects their life. This book is for those who are ready to make serious positive changes to build their EQ, manage their emotions, and increase their effectiveness in all interpersonal relationships. This is a book for those who are ready to go advanced.

Emotional Intelligence is a form of intelligence that contributes to and operates alongside your general intelligence, which is known as IQ. Psychologists and Social scientists have long realized that there are many forms of intelligence. Spouting facts and filling a chalkboard with equations are all well and good, but managing your emotions is such a powerful tool that this ability is recognized as its own form of intelligence. Emotional Intelligence isn't only the ability to manage your own emotions, but also the ability to recognize and appropriately respond to the emotions of others. Training your emotional intelligence takes work and dedication.

The last book provided some simple, practical steps to follow to begin bringing emotional intelligence concepts into your own life. The book described the many benefits of having a strong emotional intelligence. Some brief tips and tricks to begin understanding and boosting emotional intelligence include identifying and reducing negative emotional habits, engaging in active mindfulness activities, and working to identify different emotions and their processes. This book will delve deeper, drawing on proven practices to use daily in your own life to increase your emotional intelligence.

Training your emotional intelligence is not a fad diet, and it is not a quick, trivial matter. Training your emotional intelligence is a true journey. You will learn more about yourself than you ever have, and embark on a lifelong adventure. The key to building emotional intelligence is to build self-awareness. Studies show that those who actively engage in understanding and loving oneself will lead longer, happier lives. While this sounds like a large scoop of philosophical clap-trap, taking the time to be mindful of yourself is the most important thing in developing your emotional intelligence. This book will approach this topic from several angles, giving you the opportunity to find the practices that work for you and implement them.

This book will provide you with many lists and approaches to training a more effective and strong emotional intelligence. Each chapter focuses on a different aspect of emotional intelligence, and each is important to building a well-rounded EQ. The most important and recurring concept covered in this book is the notion of practice: practice, practice, practice! Every day offers you ample opportunities to practice the strategies provided in this book. Nobody ever became a master at anything without at least a little practice. Even those with a very low EQ or with very little talent in this area can achieve success through practice. The steps provided in this book are provided in a comprehensive list format, giving you specific steps to follow in a way that easy to digest.

The chapters of this book follow a chronological sequence. This means that it is not advisable to skip chapters, or to try to jump to the most advanced EQ-building strategies without building a solid foundation of EQ-building practices. Each chapter of this book is equally important, and each chapter includes a skill for you to master. Mastering each of these skills will make you a master of emotional intelligence, build your ability to improve your relationships, and control your emotions!

It is also recommended that you purchase the prequel to this book, *Emotional Intelligence: The definitive guide to understanding your emotions, how to improve your EQ and your relationships*, as a companion to this text, to gain a greater perspective on what emotional intelligence is and how it impacts your life.

Good luck on your journey to emotional intelligence mastery!

Chapter 1: Understanding the Purpose of Emotions

Those with a naturally low or untrained emotional intelligence often feel that their emotions are overwhelming and impossible to manage. In fact, society often portrays emotions as characteristics of passion: completely wild and uncontrollable. You may be surprised to find out that your emotions have a function, and they are very important to your existence and survival on this planet. Emotions may feel wild because they are relics from another time, when human lives were very different. Before you can manage your emotions, it is helpful to understand what they are, where they come from, and why they seem to take over your body and brain.

Many people seeking help with their emotional intelligence are struggling to manage what society considers "bad" or "uncomfortable" emotions. These emotions can include anger, stress, anxiety, frustration, irritation, fear, or depression and sadness. Most of these emotions exist to help you manage situations that may come into play throughout your life. Take any primate, for example, meeting a snake. Studies of monkeys confronted with a snake (even a fake one) show that the fear center of the monkey's brain, called the amygdala, lights up with activity when met with such a dangerous creature. The same studies show that the amygdala brightens, the heart rate quickens, and adrenaline enters the blood stream when that same monkey approaches an area where he or she has often seen a snake in the past, even if no snake is currently present. This is a learned response. Humans have that same brain area, the amygdala, and it also lights up when we are confronted with a fear-inducing stimulus. Anxiety and fear evolved as symptoms of a learned bodily response to situations or stimuli that may threaten our survival.

Of course, in today's world, anxiety and fear are not always symptoms of a situation that may threaten our lives. But, in a way, they are often responses to situations that may threaten our *survival*. For a businessman who has reached great success, and whose career may hinge on a certain meeting, the anxiety he feels is in response to a situation that may threaten his survival in the world of business. All of our emotions have a function that can be traced back to our initial development of survival thousands of years ago.

The purpose of your "bad" emotions is to draw your attention to whatever is happening in the present. Developing anxiety about a certain situation (like the monkey with the snake, or the businessman with his meeting) serves the function of drawing your attention to a future situation, in the hopes that you will address that situation before being confronted with it, thus contributing to your survival. Though anxiety may feel detrimental, frustrating, and even crippling, it does exist for a purpose, and that purpose is to help you navigate through a difficult life.

Understanding your emotions is vital for mastering them. What world are you trying to survive in? Do you experience a lot of anxiety, fear, depression, or anger? Which emotions make you uncomfortable? What situations lead to these emotions? Which emotions overwhelm you? These questions will be important as you move on. It is important to understand that while emotions do play a vital purpose in your life, you still have control over how you respond to those emotions. Building a great emotional intelligence is not about suppressing emotions or ridding yourself of emotions: rather, it's about identifying your emotions, tracking your responses to them, and then directing your energy into positive trends. Often those that feel overwhelmed with their emotions are those that feel powerless to act when a specific emotion takes hold. This book will train you to identify the emotions that you feel, and manage your responses to them.

Your first step in building your emotional intelligence is understanding the purpose of each emotion that you will experience. A great way to do this is to chart the emotions that you find yourself experiencing. Get out a pen and a paper to participate in this activity:

1. Write down, list style, the emotions that you feel "overwhelm" you occasionally.
2. Draw a line from each emotion. At the end of that line, write down the situations that often contribute to that emotion in your life.
3. Consider the situations that spark your emotions, and decide whether the emotions that you connected with them are rational.
4. If you feel an emotion is not rational, circle the situation that led to it.

For example, feeling anxious about exams is perfectly rational for the average student. Feeling sad about your cat passing away is also perfectly rational. How do these emotions contribute to your life? How are these emotions trying to "help" you? Anxiety about a test may encourage you to study for that test, ensuring a passing grade. Sadness about a pet's passing prepares you to deal with similar situations in the future.

Perhaps your responses to situations are not rational. For example, responding to a friend's request to go out to the movies with anger, sadness, or anxiety, is usually not a rational response. These are the emotions and situations that bear further scrutiny, which we will discuss in Chapter 2: Increasing Self-Awareness.

Keep your list of emotions and situations, and add another line following the situation for step five:

5. Identify your reactions to the emotion and situation.

This is an important step. Once you have identified emotions that you have problems with, the situations that lead to those emotions, and decided whether your emotions are rational or not, it's important to assess how you typically respond to these emotions. Do you withdraw? Do you become overly social? Do you get angry? Do you break or hit things or lash out in any other way? Finally, to complete the chapter, move to step six:

6. Decide whether your reactions are rational or not. Circle your irrational reactions.

At this point, your chart may look something like this:

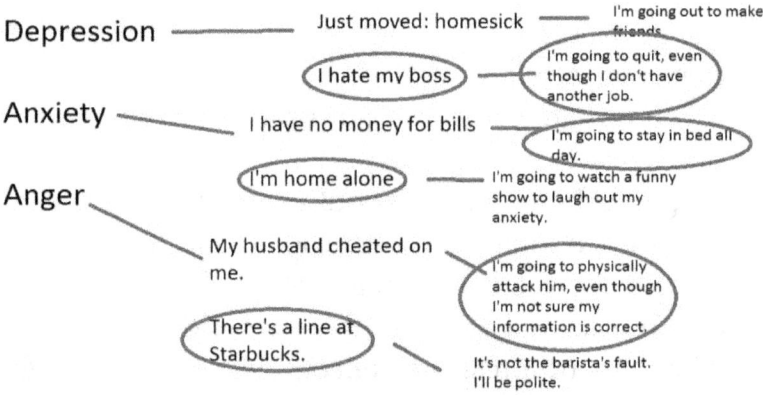

Remember that the circles indicate irrational responses: for example, extreme anxiety over being at your house alone is not a typically rational response. Deciding to physically attack someone is also not a rational response. Hold on to your chart for reference throughout the rest of the book.

Chapter 2: Increasing Your Own Self-Awareness

You've already begun your work at increasing your self-awareness in Chapter 1! The next step to managing your emotions, besides identifying their purpose and rationality, is to start developing your sense of self. You need to understand the situations that elicit your emotions, your responses to those emotions, and your reactions. To manage this, it is important to learn to be aware of yourself at all times. Self-awareness is an often-overlooked aspect of emotional intelligence. Individuals who are very self-aware are individuals who find that they communicate more effectively and honestly, are more open about who they are, and are more confident in who they are. People who are self-aware are more ready to admit to their own shortcomings, and more willing to accept criticism and amend mistakes. You can easily become highly self-aware! There are many steps you can take to make this a reality.

Engage in constant self-dialogue. This is an academic way of saying that you should talk to yourself. All the time. Every day. Engage in conversations with yourself, in your head, out loud, at your desk, in the shower. Studies show that those who talk to themselves on a consistent basis have a higher emotional intelligence and a higher general intelligence than those that do not. This is an activity that will feel strange at first. How do you talk to yourself? Start out with a simple thought: How do you (I) feel about this? Your brain will respond to the stimulus of your thought, and you will have the beginnings of a proper conversation.

Engage in mindfulness activities. Mindfulness activities can include keeping a journal, meditating consistently, and participating in activities like yoga or running. Spending time connecting with your body and mind each day will help you to build a powerful self-awareness. Each of these activities forces you to slow down and focus solely on yourself for a period of time, without constant outside distractions. You may be surprised to find what you'll learn about yourself.

Take a personality test. Who are you, psychologically speaking? What does the research have to say about people who share your traits? Personality tests are created to tell you what your personality means for you and your life. Many individuals are surprised by what a personality test tells them: many are less so. Personality tests are organized specifically so that you cannot "cheat" the test to get the personality you want—so it's best to answer every question openly and honestly! A personality test can highlight your strengths and reveal weaknesses in a concise and straightforward manner. Many personality tests include advice for you and your personality type. What does your personality mean going forward? How best is your personality managed? Personality tests are easily accessible online, and many are free!

Reflect on your history. This is a step that is not intuitive, and many people don't think to include their life history in their daily self-reflections. Most modern psychologists agree that both genetics and life history shape the people that we become. This means that much of who you are is innate, but a lot of who you are is shaped, like clay. Consider where you've come from and what has happened throughout your life. Take the time to consider minute details in addition to the major ones. Ask yourself what major challenges you've conquered, and what major obstacles have defeated you. Consider your major achievements. Also consider your average daily life as a child, teenager, and adult. Think back to the smallest details, like what you had for lunch every day in Kindergarten. Did your caregivers dress you, or did you dress yourself? Were you shy, or were you outspoken and loud? Did you have many friends? Did you have more friends at one time in your life than at another? Did you suffer any major losses? Picking apart your history is likely to take longer than a Saturday afternoon. Spend time thinking on this topic whenever you take a little time to reflect.

Notice signs from your body. When a situation confronts you, track the way that your body reacts to it. In Chapter 1, you worked on tracking specific emotions and the situations that elicit them. Now, it is important to notice your bodily reactions to a specific situation. This is a good place to re-examine the chart that you created in Chapter 1. Take in the emotions you feel are a problem and the situations that you wrote down. It's a good idea to consider every situation that you put down, but an especially good idea to consider the ones that you circled as "irrational." Think to one of these situations, and consider what happened to your body when you were confronted with the emotional problem. Did your heart speed up? Did you start to hyperventilate? Did you grow dizzy? Did your body feel hot or cold? Did your muscles tense? As you move forward, take the time to notice your body when you are feeling uncomfortable emotionally. Notice what emotions are doing to you physically, so you can be better prepared to deal with the situations later on.

Taking the time to focus on yourself and recognize your own triggers and responses is an effective way to begin building your emotional intelligence. Building self-awareness is a vital step, and can be achieved by simply spending time with yourself. This chapter identified a few ways that you can accomplish this goal, but the list included in this chapter is not exhaustive. Finding constructive ways to spend time reflecting in your own way is never a negative action. Perhaps you enjoy going to the nail salon and relaxing over a pedicure? This can be a great place to reflect. Or perhaps you bicycle to work? Turn the headphones to background music and spend your morning ride conversing with yourself. Your entire day is full of opportunities to get to know the person inside your head, if you only take the time to notice those moments.

Chapter 3: Reducing Negative habits

Now that you have spent some time in self-reflection and emotion identification, it is time to work on recognizing and reducing negative emotional and behavioral trends. Negative pattern replacement is the next vital step in building your emotional intelligence. First, you must identify negative behavioral and emotional trends. Then, you must identify positive behavioral and emotional trends. Finally, you must strive to replace negative habits with positive ones, or at least reduce the occurrence of the negative habits.

Negative behavioral and emotional trends stem from places of deep insecurity, anger, depression, or frustration. Negative emotional habits can include blaming behaviors, anger, and jealousy. In this chapter, we're going to discuss the deeper issues that create negative behavioral and emotional trends, and strive to eliminate them, or replace them with positive behaviors, so that you can move away from negative habits once and for all.

First, you must identify negative habits in your own life. Do you often engage in blaming others for situational stress? Do you lash out in anger without meaning to? Do you seek attention to feel satisfaction? Take the time to really confront the negative habits that you engage in when interacting with others. A good way to do this is to get the information out on paper, as you've done in Chapters 1 and 2. First, retrieve your Emotions and Situations chart. Notice the reactions section, where you have circled your irrational reactions. Take note of the irrational reactions that you circled. You're going to begin a new activity, and to do so, you'll need a separate sheet of paper and a pencil or a pen.

1. Make a list. Write down the irrational reactions that you circled on your

Emotions and Situations chart.

2. Now, spend some time reflecting, purely on emotional conflicts and situations with others. What other irrational reactions have you engaged in, if any? Add these to your list.

3. Once you have run out of irrational reactions, write down your most common reactions, whether they are irrational or rational.

4. Now, take a look at your list. Is there any sort of pattern emerging? Do you have a tendency to react in anger? Do you retreat? What do you see?

5. After examining your list, in a separate column, write down your observations about your behavior. What negative behaviors might you be engaging in?

For some, this kind of self-reflection can be difficult, and identifying your own trends of behavior can seem impossible! If this is the case for you, then after trying this activity, you can seek more comprehensive help. In Chapter 2 we discussed the idea of taking a personality test. Now, to get to know your own negative emotional and behavioral trends, it's a good idea to turn to the people in your life to ask them for their opinions. Using online resources, you can either construct or purchase a simple, anonymous test for your friends and relatives to create a comprehensive picture of your trends. This is called a 360 degree test. This is a great way to receive constructive criticism without feeling hurt or angry or causing a confrontation with the members of your family. The data is presented comprehensively and anonymously, giving you good information. Once again, you should get out that pen and paper, and write down the negative habits that you spot emerging in your own life.

Once you have identified your major negative emotional habits, it is time to reduce, replace, or even eliminate these trends altogether. Negative habits have a major effect in your life and on your emotional intelligence. You can eliminate them by remaining mindful of the problem and constantly working for change.

Stay cognizant of situations that provoke negative emotional habits. Stay alert! If you know that a situation typically triggers an adverse pattern from you, pay attention and identify the situation early on. You can do this by remaining mindful at all times, by considering which situations trigger you during your self-reflection moments, or by making a concrete list as you've been doing throughout the book.

Remove yourself from triggering situations. If you know that a situation provokes a negative emotional or behavioral pattern, remove yourself from it before your emotions and behaviors can get out of control.

Express yourself. If a situation or even a specific person often initiate a negative emotional or behavioral pattern in your life, express your struggle. It isn't wrong to be struggling with negative habits, and you are a stronger person for trying to fight them.

Build a support system. If the important people in your life know and understand that you are trying to make positive changes, they can get involved and help you toward your goal. Just like joining an exercise group for support in losing weight, utilizing your friends and family to help you through your emotional struggle is hugely beneficial. Family and friends can help you identify your negative habits, calmly point them out as they are happening, and help you form strategies to avoid the problems in the future.

Negative habits are a lifelong struggle for most people. By implementing the steps outlined in this chapter, you can effectively reduce or even eliminate these trends in your own life. By doing so, you have now opened up your ability to focus on your own positive emotions, your reactions to your emotions, and your ability to notice and interpret others' emotions and reactions. These are all important steps in the journey to building a higher emotional intelligence. By implementing these steps, you open the door to further mastering your emotions and improving your interpersonal relationships on a massive scale.

Chapter 4: Stress Management

One of the most difficult and overwhelming emotions to manage in today's modern world is stress. Studies show that stress in individuals living in industrialized societies has increased on a massive, almost epidemic scale over the past century. Stress is a very real problem, and it increases chemicals in your body like cortisol that can have a very detrimental impact on your brain and your body in large amounts. People who are overwhelmed by stress are often plagued by sleeplessness, depression, listlessness, lack of libido, and disinterest in the things they used to love. In simple terms, stress makes people unhappy and life unenjoyable. Unfortunately, massive amounts of stress can lead to life-changing problems in health. High levels of stress have been linked to rises in obesity, heart disease, mental illness, and even increases in cancer. Stress itself can take lives: massive levels of stress among student populations in industrialized countries have been linked to rising rates of suicide. Unfortunately, in many Westernized societies, stress is not seen as the significant health issue that it is, and many adult individuals are expected to cope with their stress quietly. The inability to manage stress is often seen as a character deficiency, which it is not. This chapter will teach you how to manage the stress in your own life, bringing it down to manageable levels. Managing your stress will help you to reduce overwhelming emotions as a whole, increasing your emotional intelligence.

Avoid artificial substances like caffeine, alcohol, or nicotine. If your stress levels are high, treating them with caffeine, alcohol, or nicotine is not the answer! Putting these substances into your body will only have a detrimental effect on your body's natural rhythm, making your stress more intense. Also, studies show that self-treating high stress levels with addictive substances like these increase your likelihood of becoming addicted and facing a lifelong addiction. If you are already dealing with an addiction, try to cut down to one "fix" per day, before slowly tapering off your usage. Quitting "cold turkey" can lead to an oppressive cycle of abuse and withdrawal that can plague you for years to come.

Sleep, sleep, sleep, and sleep some more! The studies are conclusive on this one! More sleep makes for a happier individual. Cutting out sleep to get more work done is terrible for your health and will lead to much more stress in the long run. If you can't squeeze in the time to sleep at night, then try to find time to take a "power nap" during the day. More sleep allows your brain to reset and process more information. A rested brain is a brain that is more ready to deal with life's challenges, especially stress management, emotional management, and social interaction. A lack of sleep can lead to an increase in anxiety, stress, and depression, while simultaneously decreasing your overall health. If there is one positive change that you have room for in your life, make it this one. Sleep is vital!

Seek problem-solving techniques. Stress is often stimulated by being presented with a problem that we feel we are unable to solve. Often this leads to anxiety over the problem, or even an avoidance of the problem, which in turn leads to a significant increase in stress and even more difficulty confronting the problem. Learning to solve problems quickly and efficiently gives you a stronger feeling of control over your life, which will in turn reduce your overall stress levels. One great way to approach a problem is to write down the problem, and then write down as many solutions as possible (even the crazy ones!) as they pop into your head. This is a great way to think outside the box and get out of your own head, so that you can take a new angle in problem-solving.

Relearn phrases like "No!" and "I won't!" or even "I can't!" These are favorite phrases of toddlers and preschoolers all over the world, but as we grow these phrases are trained out of us. We are taught to say "yes," to put in 100% of our effort at all times. We are taught that good workers do not decline assignments or opportunities, and good people should be willing to do things for others. Well, adding more to your plate is increasing your stress, and when it comes to your health, it's okay to put yourself first. It's time to start evaluating your commitments and deciding which are priorities and which are not. It's important to learn that it is okay to decline a commitment, and it is okay to tell others "no!" Reducing your workload is a great way to reduce your stress, and it's a step that is often overlooked.

Exercise. The notion of getting more exercise has returned time and time again in our discussion of increasing emotional intelligence, and it's because, other than sleep, exercise is the greatest cure for any emotional or mental struggles you are dealing with. Exercise increases your overall health, increasing your body's efficiency and your brain's ability to process and manage information and emotions. More exercise allows you to build that body-brain connection that we discussed in Chapter 2, which is a great step in increasing your overall emotional intelligence.

Give yourself a break. There is no shame in allowing yourself time in the evening or morning to watch television, have a cup of coffee, or go for a run. Taking time to yourself is a great way to reduce overall stress, increase self-awareness, and build emotional intelligence.

As you reduce stress in your life, you free up more processing power for managing emotions and connecting with others. Stress is often a key player in the negative emotional and behavioral trends that we discussed in Chapter 3. By reducing overall stress, you increase your health, your overall intelligence, and your ability to process complex emotions and situations.

Chapter 5: The "Bounce Back" Effect

Now that you have begun the extensive journey into self-discovery, awareness, reflection, and emotional and behavioral management, it is time for you to build the traits of an individual with a high emotional intelligence. This chapter and the following chapters will give you new abilities that you may not have implemented into your life in the past. It is very important that you successfully implement strategies from chapters 1 through 4 before attempting to throw new behaviors into your life. Self-reflection and discovery, along with emotional management, are the first and most important steps in building a stronger emotional intelligence.

Once you feel that you have made good progress on these concepts, it's time to add some new behaviors. This chapter discusses the idea of the "Bounce Back" Effect. Those with a high emotional intelligence often show a strong ability to "bounce back" from adversity. This means that, when confronted with difficult situations, those with a high emotional intelligence are able to process the adverse situation, manage the emotions elicited by the situation, and move on without allowing the situation to significantly impact their life. Building a high emotional intelligence can enable you to bounce back from some of life's most difficult challenges: divorce, break-ups, loss of a job, weight gain, illness, or even loss of a loved one. The ability to do this will significantly increase your life satisfaction and is a major trait of a strong emotional intelligence.

How do you manage it? How do you simply bounce back from a major problem? Well, you can begin by practicing with the smaller problems in your life. Did terrible traffic put you in a bad mood on your way to work? Did you get into a fight with your significant other? Utilize the steps listed in this chapter to overcome small challenges, working your way up to life's more difficult experiences.

Gain some perspective. When the problems begin, it is often easy to fall into the trap of allowing our emotions to get out of hand. Try to look at the problem objectively. How has this problem really impacted your life? Is it actually the end of the world? Is it possible to survive? If needed, make a list of the real problems that this situation creates for you, and then implement problem-solving strategies to address each one. By working through the situation methodically, you can keep your emotions in check and move on.

Focus on the future. Focusing on the problem and on the past situation is a great way to increase your stress and depression surrounding the issue. Instead of looking at the problem, focus on the future. How does this situation change what can and will happen in the future? How does it affect your plans? How can you adjust your plans to reach your goals? Is it time to set new goals? By focusing on planning and on an approach to your goals, you allow yourself to adjust to the situation and move on from it.

Focus on the positives. This is a very important strategy that is reused again and again by mental health professionals. What have you gained from this negative situation? What new opportunities or pathways have opened for you? What do you still have in your life? What is good? Focus on the things that make you happy, and on being grateful for them, to avoid dwelling on the negative impact of the situation that you are facing.

Avoid using absolutes. If you think about your situation in terms of absolutes, you allow it to grow into a much larger problem than it needs to be. Absolutes are words like "never" or "forever" or "always." Saying things like, "I'll never be happy again!" or "This ALWAYS happens to me!" are absolute phrases that allow your emotions to overwhelm you. Consider the problem logically. Does this really always happen? When was the last time that it didn't?

Build a support system. As always, when managing emotions, stress, or negative situations, a support system is key. There is never shame in asking for the help of others, and connecting with other people allows you to move away from your problems for a bit. Discussing your problems out loud and receiving advice from loved ones is also an excellent way to process emotion and build a plan for the future.

Stay busy. When dealing with an extremely difficult problem, it is best to stay busy doing things that you enjoy. Take up a new hobby or exercise program. Keeping your mind and body active prevents you from dwelling on the issue and allows you to move on more effectively.

Seek professional help. For life's extremely difficult situations, like divorce, break-ups, illness, or loss of a loved one, seeking the opinion and advice of a mental health professional is always a good idea. A mental health professional can help you to identify problem behaviors and triggers, and help you to work your way through the challenge that life has presented to you. A mental health professional is also in an excellent position to offer information on support groups. A professionally organized support group is a way to connect with others who are experiencing the same challenge that you are dealing with. Attending a professional support group allows you to know that you are not alone, and gives you the perspectives of others in dealing with your challenges.

Bouncing back is not a quick skill to learn, but by using these steps to approach challenges in your life, it's a skill that you can build over time. Life will always come with challenges, large and small, and there will be ample opportunities to practice. This leads to our last piece of advice on the matter: when dealing with adversity, approach each situation as a new challenge and opportunity to implement your skills. By approaching the situation as a challenge and looking at it objectively, you minimize its emotional impact and maximize your ability to deal with it.

Chapter 6: Expressing Complex Emotions

Emotional intelligence is not only about managing emotions as they threaten to overwhelm you, but also about the ability to express you emotions in a constructive way to others. Expressing emotions, especially complex emotions, can be a difficult process for a lot of people. Many individuals develop an inner fear of expressing their emotions that lead to significant negative habits and an inability to properly communicate with others. To build a strong emotional intelligence, it is vital that you learn to express emotions. This chapter will cut straight to the heart of the issue, teaching you to identify and express your most complex emotions in a healthy and constructive way.

Chapter 1 discussed the fact that emotions are physiological processes that influence our bodies and are influenced by our thought processes. Studies show that strong emotions can supercharge your body, drawing on energy stores and giving you an energy "boost." While this may sound like a positive effect, it most often becomes a problem when individuals choose not to express their emotions. Many individuals will attempt to suppress their emotions, allowing unresolved feelings to build until they become too complex to explain in a calm manner. This can lead to outbursts of fear, anxiety, or anger. Outbursts are an unhealthy method of communication, and can lead to unhealthy interpersonal relationships. It is important to express your emotions early on, so that they do not build in this way.

Identify what you are feeling. The first and most complicated step in expressing your difficult emotions is to identify the emotion in the first place. This is often easier said than done. As children, we heard words like "mad" or "angry" or "sad" or "frustrated." But as adults, our emotions become too complex for such simple words. Consider the possibility that you may be feeling more than one emotion at a time. To identify what you are feeling, consider an emotion tracker. You can use a paper-and-pen journal version, writing down what you feel as you feel it, or there are many cell phone apps and mental health websites that will allow you to update your emotion quickly and easily from a given list. The lists on these apps are often extensive, providing you with options you may not have considered.

Track your emotions. Everyone has bad days. Some days, you may feel extremely angry, extremely depressed, or extremely frustrated. Without keeping a log of your emotions, you may start to feel that you are depressed all the time, or angry all the time. It is easy to lose track of what you were feeling and when you were feeling it. By tracking your emotions, using a journal or an emotion tracking app, you can pay attention to what emotions you feel frequently, and what triggers them.

Identify the source of your emotions. Are you frequently angry around a particular person or place? Is there a specific person that makes you too happy for words? Hone in on emotions that you feel on a regular basis, and take note of the situations that make you feel that way. Identify any people who are involved in your emotional process, and figure out what their role is in your emotional day.

Before communicating, decide on a goal. What do you hope to achieve by communicating your emotions to another person? There are many motives for communicating an emotion. You may need attention or recognition. You may be looking for guidance. You may be seeking reciprocity. You may simply need to express yourself to get the emotions out. Decide on what your goal is with your communication, and take time to evaluate your goal. Is this a positive behavior? Is your goal fair?

Make a plan. All emotional communication does not need to be a lengthy process, but you should take at least a brief moment to plan how you would like to communicate. Do you communicate best in person? Do you communicate best through technology, as in texting or email? Do you communicate best through writing with pen and paper? When expressing emotions, there is no "wrong" method of communication, and it is up to you to decide what is best for you.

Now that you are ready to express yourself, the following steps will help you to ensure that your expression of emotions is healthy and constructive. Remember, remaining in control at all times is the key to effectively expressing your emotions.

Avoid blaming. When expressing complicated emotions, especially negative ones, it is easy to blame the other party for the way that you are feeling. Blaming behaviors are not constructive, and are a well-known negative behavioral pattern.

Use "I feel" statements. To keep your communication effective, highlight that the way you're feeling is just that: a feeling. These are emotions that you are communicating. This guideline is helpful for preventing blaming behaviors. It is easy to say "You make me angry when…", but it isn't constructive. Rather, using a statement like "I felt very angry when…" places the emphasis on your feelings rather than on the actions of another person.

Express your goal. When communicating your feelings, it is important to identify why you are feeling the need to express these emotions. Otherwise, the other individual(s) may feel that you are trying to attack them. They may react defensively to your words, rather than listening and responding in a constructive manner. A good way to do this is to start out with your goal when expressing yourself. Start out your communication by saying something like, "I really feel the need to express how I've been feeling to you, because I'm learning that allowing emotions to build is unhealthy." Or, you could say "I want to express how [incident] made me feel, so that we can connect like we used to."

Adjust your expectations and accept helplessness. You are in control of yourself and of your emotions. You are not in control of the emotions of another person, nor are you in control of their reactions. It is not healthy to enter into a communication with the expectation that the other person will respond a certain way. By forcing this expectation on the other individual, you may sabotage the entire communication and set yourself up for failure or disappointment. For example, perhaps you are about to tell a significant other "I love you" for the first time. You cannot enter the communication expecting them to respond the same way. If you are saying "I love you" only to hear the words returned, then this is not a healthy or constructive communication.

Prepare an exit strategy. The steps provided in this chapter are intended to assist you in maintaining control over your communication of your complex emotions, but you cannot have control over the entire communication process. If you feel that you are becoming overwhelmed, and that the communication is no longer constructive, then it is important to be able to leave the communication and re-evaluate the situation. For example, if the communication has devolved into shouting or even into physical violence, it is no longer constructive and it is time to leave. Before entering into the communication, prepare yourself for the possibility that you may need to exit, and prepare a plan for that possibility. Make sure that you have a way out. Knowing that you can leave at any time also gives you an additional measure of control over the situation.

Allow your body to respond to your emotions. Your body has its own way of expressing emotions. When expressing yourself to other individuals, it is easy to feel that you may need to cry, or to stand and pace, or to embrace the person you're communicating with. Do not fight these urges, as this is a form of suppressing your emotions! Allowing your body to freely express itself should not be a measure of shame.

Leave no room for fear. Expressing deep and complex emotions can be a frightening process. Do not allow fear to stand in your way! If you feel afraid, practice relaxation techniques. Take in slow, deep breaths, breathing in through your nose and out through your mouth. Remind yourself why it is more beneficial to express your emotions than it is to hold them in.

Expressing complex emotions can be a daunting process, but like any aspect of emotional intelligence building, this step can be conquered with practice and determination. It is okay to start small, working on expressing the little things that you feel throughout the day before moving on to expressing the larger feelings that are overwhelming your life. Remember, holding your emotions in is never the answer!

Chapter 7: Handling Intimacy

There are two different kinds of intimacy: emotional intimacy and physical intimacy. Because human bodies are designed to focus on reproduction, physical intimacy is often much more easily accomplished than emotional intimacy. In a strong romantic relationship, emotional intimacy and physical intimacy combine, allowing two people to be intimate with each other in every way. Unfortunately, many relationships are weakened by an inability to form a strong bond through emotional intimacy. This chapter will teach you how to bring emotional intimacy into your life in a healthy, constructive manner.

Emotional intimacy is frightening. To reach true emotional intimacy, you must allow yourself to be very vulnerable, which is a terrifying thought for many individuals. Vulnerability is nearly impossible for those who have deep-rooted self-esteem problems or deep fears of rejection. If these problems are large issues for you, then it is important that you spend a significant amount of time working through chapters 1 through 4, engaging in self-reflection and confidence-building. To be emotionally intimate and vulnerable with another person, you must build a measure of self-confidence. You must have the knowledge that, should the intimacy fail, you can survive and support yourself emotionally. Once you feel that you are confident enough to initiate emotional intimacy, follow the steps in this chapter to guide you to success.

Establish boundaries for safety. Emotional intimacy is dependent on the feeling of safety. It's important to know that, when getting close with another person, you are safe. Your body is constantly attuned to your safety, both emotionally and physically, and you should pay attention to its cues. If you feel unsafe, or feel that something isn't right, then you should address that intuition. Otherwise, ensure clear boundaries are defined in your relationship to facilitate healthy intimacy.

Build trust. When working to build emotional intimacy, it is vitally important that you are able to trust the other person involved. Trust must usually be built over time. You will find that you can trust another individual after repeated interactions that demonstrate trustworthy behavior. The more trust you build, the deeper your connection will go.

Focus on face-to-face interaction. Put away the phone, the tablet, and the laptop. True emotional intimacy is best built with good, old-fashioned, face-to-face communication. You may feel that you can express yourself just as well—or even more effectively—through online, texting, or written communication. However, the healthiest way to build a truly intimate emotional relationship is still through in-person interaction. Studies show that 93% of human communication is nonverbal. When you are interacting with another individual, you are picking up constant subtle cues. Without realizing it, you notice how dilated the person's eyes are, how fast the pulse is beating in their neck, and the slightest tick of their facial muscles. Every aspect of the person's body gives you information that feeds the communication. This type of communication is most effective for building an emotionally intimate relationship.

Move slowly. Building emotional intimacy is a process, and it must be allowed to happen naturally. Trying to force emotional intimacy will quickly derail your progress. To manage this, try expressing a small amount of yourself at a time. For some, it is easy to express too much, and tell someone everything about you all at once. This can be difficult for another person to process, and difficult for them to respond to. Instead, focus on small aspects of your personality, allowing the other person to learn about you bit by bit, until they are able to see a much bigger picture. In this way, they can process all of the bits of information about you, instead of feeling overwhelmed.

What if I've been hurt before? If emotional intimacy has become a problem for you after dealing with a negative experience, it can be easy to focus on that experience and obsess over similarities with a new person. You may quickly begin to feel that the situation is dangerous based on similarities with a past situation. To combat this, try to focus on how this person is different from the last. If you want to get out your pen and paper to make a list, that would be a good idea. Write down the many things that you have noticed that set this person apart from others you've tried to get close to. By focusing on these differences, you can set yourself and ease and facilitate the building of intimacy.

Separate emotional and physical intimacy. Do not confuse these two forms of intimacy. Physical intimacy with another individual is not a guarantee of trust or safety. It is important to remember that emotional intimacy is separate from physical intimacy, and must grow in its own way and from its own process.

Allow intimacy to be fun! Building emotional intimacy doesn't always need to be a serious endeavor. Plan some activities with this person, things that you enjoy, and bring them into your world by introducing them to your hobbies and activities. Connecting over an activity is a great way to relax while opening up about yourself.

Emotional intimacy takes a lot of time to form. Some studies show that it is impossible to fully know another individual until you've known them for a full two years or more! Knowing that emotional intimacy cannot be rushed gives you the room you need to relax and take your time with building a strong foundation of trust, boundaries, and safety. Emotional intimacy is often a terrifying prospect, but by taking this process one step at a time, you set yourself up to succeed. Building strong emotional intimacy is a great skill that will provide you with emotional benefits throughout your life. Honing this skill is an important part of building a stronger and more effective emotional intelligence.

Chapter 8: Managing Your Reactions

As you begin building stronger relationships with others, it is important to take a step back and once again evaluate your interactions with others. Specifically, it is important to evaluate the way that you react to interactions with other people. Previously in the book, we discussed managing reactions to emotions like fear, anxiety, and stress. This is an important skill that will help you when working through this chapter. Now, it is time to work on managing your reactions to other people. When interacting with others, you are constantly being presented with stimuli—words, touch, body language—and your reactions can have a massive impact on the flow of the conversation. When your reactions are negative, and impact the communication in a non-constructive way, then you are effecting your ability to communicate with others as well as your ability to form long-term interpersonal relationships. This chapter will provide you with the steps you need to identify your reactions and manage them in your daily interpersonal communications.

In previous chapters, we discussed identifying emotions and expressing them. Often, negative reactions in your daily life and communication with others stem from emotions that overwhelm you in the moment. A stimulus causes you to feel emotional, you are overwhelmed by that emotion, and you react in a non-constructive manner. If this is the case, then the steps in previous chapters will go a long way in helping you to identify the feelings that cause you to feel overwhelmed and to react. When managing your reactions with others, it is important to understand what a reaction is. A reaction is your choice to express your emotions in a specific time or place without logical reason. Managing reactions can be difficult and frustrating, but with practice, this is a skill that you can master.

Accept that your reactions are solely your responsibility. This is the first and most important step in learning to manage your reactions. Taking responsibility for your actions is like admitting you have a problem: you can't make a change without accepting responsibility. Accepting responsibility places you in a position of power over your reactions and emotions. These are yours to control: you are not a victim.

Identify the physical signs of an emotional reaction. In previous chapters, we discussed building an awareness of the body and of emotions' impacts on your physiological processes. An emotional reaction often stems from an overwhelming bodily response. As a reminder, signs of a physical emotional reaction can include a racing heartbeat, sweaty palms, fast breathing, stomach fluttering, an overall jitteriness, or muscle tension. Recognize these signs so that you can remain in control of your thought process while your body reacts.

Focus on what caused your emotional reaction. How are you feeling, and why are you feeling this way? What part of your personality is causing you to react in this way? For example, say you are at work and are planning on heading out the door in five minutes. Your boss approaches you and informs you that you will need to stay for another two hours because an avoidable situation has come up. You react in anger and lash out at your boss. What could cause you to react this way? In this situation, you were excited about going home. The sudden disappointment presented by your boss caused you to feel overwhelmed with disappointment, which led to a feeling of bitterness, which was facilitated by a blaming behavior, which resulted in anger toward your boss and your reaction. Identifying what caused you to feel the way that you do can help you to measure your reaction and respond appropriately.

Make a decision about how you choose to feel, and how you choose to respond. Remember, your emotions are under your control. You do not have to choose to be angry, or sad, or depressed. Using the above example, the initial emotion felt was disappointment. After the disappointment caused you to feel overwhelmed, you chose to allow anger into your mindset. Remember to always focus on the positive: you can choose to respond in a positive way. You are in control.

Actively adjust your perspective and attitude. Once you have chosen the best course for your response to the situation, it is time to take a moment and actively adjust. First, allow yourself a moment to relax. Take in several long, slow, deep breaths, breathing in through the nose and out through the mouth. Allow your mind to let go of the situation and the thoughts that are still racing through. Once your mind has cleared and your heartbeat has slowed, take a moment to center yourself. You can achieve this by placing your feet slightly apart, balancing well, and drawing your attention to your center of gravity. Once you feel calm and present, you can focus on your new objective. If you have decided not to respond in a negative way, focus on a goal for your response. Do not focus on the stimuli that caused you to react emotionally, but rather focus on what you now plan to do.

When all else fails, *smile*. Sometimes a situation beyond your control will hit you without warning and force you to respond immediately. You may not have time to measure your reaction, evaluate your feelings, or center yourself. When this happens, the moment you feel the emotional reaction taking over your body, plaster a smile onto your face. It may be the fakest smile you have ever smiled, but it will help. Studies show that smiling itself increases happiness in the moment. The old saying, "fake it till you make it" holds a measure of truth! Responding quickly with a smile enables you to quickly gain control over your reaction and buy yourself time to slow your reaction down.

Your reactions can be a major obstacle in interpersonal communication. A major trait in those who have a high emotional intelligence is an ability to manage their reactions and responses to emotional stimuli. By practicing the steps presented in this chapter, you can gradually build this skill and master this aspect of your emotional intelligence.

Chapter 9: Emotions in Others

An upper-level characteristic of those who are masters in emotional intelligence is the ability to accurately read, respond to, and even manipulate emotions in others. Often, communication with others is hindered by an inability to accurately read and respond to their emotions. Many individuals are so tuned-in to how they themselves would show emotion in a particular situation that they are unable to identify different ways of expressing emotion. When you cannot identify with someone else's expression of emotion, you are likely to misinterpret their intentions, leading to a botched communication. This chapter will present some key aspects of emotional expression that are somewhat universal in Western cultures. This essential guide will help you to read emotions in others, which in turn will help you to effectively respond.

Pay attention to body cues. As mentioned in Chapter 9, 93% of human communication are nonverbal. There are specific cues that indicate certain emotions.

- Distance: Note where the person is standing or sitting while speaking to you. Are they leaning toward you, or are they leaning away? Studies show that sitting closer to a person, and leaning toward them, are signs that the person likes that individual.
- Hand placement: Where an individual places their hands can say a lot about their motivations during an interaction. For example, if you are interacting with a person who chooses to hide their hands, this is an indication that they are holding something back. This doesn't necessarily indicate a hostile intent—they may be withholding emotions that they are scared to express,

or they may simply feel uncomfortable.
- Arm and leg placement: When an individual crosses their arms or crosses their legs, or both, this is an indication that this person feels angry, uncomfortable, or even defensive. Of course, they could also be cold.
- Fidgeting and picking: When an individual cannot sit still, or is picking at parts of their body (playing with hair, chewing nails, biting lips) this is an indication that this person is feeling awkward. Picking and fidgeting are psychological processes that developed to self-soothe.

Pay attention to facial expressions. The face is an open book for you to read! The human face is capable of forming many different kinds of expressions, and learning to interpret them will enable you to pay attention to the emotions of others. Most angry and uncomfortable expressions will take on some form of frown, while happy and eager expressions take on some form of smile.

Learn the habits of specific individuals. By paying attention to physical cues each time you interact with an individual in your life, you build the skills to interpret their body language later on. Do your sister's eyes dart around the room when she lies? Does your husband look at the floor when he is uncomfortable? Does your girlfriend laugh to hide the fact that she is angry?

Take the time to notice potential emotional cues. This is a form of putting yourself in the other individual's shoes. What aspects of the current situation might elicit feelings in the person you're communicating with? Perhaps your boss is being uncharacteristically rude today. What may be happening in his life right now? Perhaps, while on a first date, you notice a girl leaning away from you while fidgeting. These are signs of feeling awkward. Is something about the situation cueing this behavior?

Accept others' rights to their own emotions. Remember that everyone deals with emotional stimuli, as you have been struggling throughout this book. Not everyone will feel the same emotions in response to the same triggers that you will. It is important to recognize the right of others to feel, and to recognize that this is outside of your control.

Monitor your own reactions and responses. In the last chapter, you learned how to monitor your own emotional reactions and responses. A strong emotional cue can be realizing the emotions of others. If, for example, your boss is being rude today, it can be difficult not to react in kind. However, once you've accepted the right of others to their emotions, you need to remind yourself that reacting to these emotions is not constructive.

Engage in active listening. There may be times that individuals in your life seek to express their own emotions to you, as you learned how to do in Chapter 6. Remember your own reservations over emotional interactions, and give this person the courtesy that you would want when expressing yourself. Expressing emotions can be difficult for everyone, and for you to effectively identify and respond to the emotions of others, active listening is key.

Identifying emotions in others is another skill that takes time to build, but luckily, there are opportunities for practice everywhere! You can even make it into a game. When at a restaurant, or at the grocery store, observe other individuals and teach yourself to identify their emotions from their body language. By training your eyes to notice the smallest details, you will build this skill quickly and become an emotional professional.

Chapter 10: Taking Responsibility: Taking Control

Now that you have mastered the advanced steps toward building a strong and powerful emotional intelligence, it's time to adjust your mindset in managing your emotions. As briefly discussed in previous chapters, a characteristic of those with a strong emotional intelligence is the ability to take responsibility for your emotions. In many industrialized societies, emotions are characterized as negative symptoms that are uncontrollable. Many individuals with a poor emotional intelligence have the mindset that emotions are outside their control, and this leads to permission-seeking behaviors. This negative behavioral pattern is the pattern of identifying as a victim, so that you may gain attention to engage in negative habits again and again. Have you ever used the words, "I'm sorry this happened, but I just got so angry!"? Or perhaps you've used a phrase such as, "I couldn't help it, I was just frustrated." These are phrases that highlight permissive-seeking behaviors. To truly build a strong emotional intelligence, you must realize that you are not a victim to your emotions.

To accomplish this, you must take responsibility for your emotions, for your reactions, and for your responses. You must recognize that it is truly you who are in control over how you feel and how you choose to respond to a specific stimulus. This can be a daunting task, and it's easy to slip into the pattern of blaming your emotions for your behaviors. By taking responsibility for your emotions, you are shifting the blame to yourself. This is an important step, because it places you in a position of control. When you feel that you have lost control or responded to a situation in an adverse or negative manner, it is your responsibility to evaluate what happened and prevent the situation from re-occurring. Your emotions are in your hands. Your emotional intelligence is in your control.

In this book, you have learned that emotional intelligence is something that can be trained. Therefore, it is your responsibility to train your emotional intelligence. You have been given the knowledge, and now it is up to you to implement the steps and procedures provided in this book. You cannot return to the belief that your emotions are out of your control. You cannot subscribe to the idea that you are a victim to your emotions. You can train yourself to be in control, and you must take responsibility over that training. This practice, like any other practice described in this book, can be accomplished with repeated practice of some simple steps.

Begin each day with intent. Each day, make a decision. Decide that today, you are responsible for your emotions. Decide that you are responsible for your reactions. Tell yourself that you are in control, and you intend to remain in control.

State your intentions to a partner or a friend. By claiming your responsibility out loud, you officially gain ownership over your emotions and reactions. By bringing someone else into your intention to take responsibility, you are forcing yourself to be accountable to this person.

Constantly engage in mindfulness. Mindfulness is the root of emotional intelligence building. Spending time getting to know yourself and understanding your own thoughts, emotions, and processes is never a bad thing. Remember to actively engage in mindfulness strategies on a daily basis to maintain control over your emotional situation.

Practice taking responsibility. After a situation of dealing with overwhelming emotions, take ownership. If you did well, congratulate yourself. If you were unsuccessful, make a plan to be more effective when the situation repeats itself.

Trust yourself! You can do this. Tell yourself that you can do this, and remind yourself that you are in control. Building a strong emotional intelligence takes time, and you are well down the road to emotional intelligence mastery.

Taking responsibility over your emotions and reactions puts you in control over yourself and puts you in the driver's seat. This is your journey, and you are in control. Take ownership of that!

Conclusion

Congratulations! You have completed this text on emotional intelligence mastery. By completing each of the steps outlined in each of the chapters of this book, you are well on your way to mastering your emotional intelligence, massively improving your interpersonal relationships, and controlling your emotions. Remember that practice is key: practicing each of these concepts will make you a true master in all of these areas.

You are now ready to take on the world of emotional stimuli by utilizing the steps provided by this book. As you do so, pay attention: what works for you? Not every step will work for every person in every situation. This is an excellent opportunity for you to experiment. As you begin practicing, take a note of how the steps provided by this book impact your life. Take note of what works most effectively for you and what doesn't, and adjust your practices based on these findings. It is time for you to become your own scientist, investigating your own life and your own needs. Every individual and everyone's emotional intelligence needs are unique!

As you move forward, if you find that this book has been effective in increasing your emotional intelligence, improving your interpersonal relationships, and gaining control over your emotions, consider using the prequel to this book, *Emotional Intelligence: The Definitive Guide to Understanding Your Emotions, How to Improve Your EQ and Your Relationships*, to further increase your knowledge on the topic.

If these books have benefited you, please leave a review on amazon so that others may begin their journey!

If you feel that this book is an effective guide to building your emotional intelligence, consider sharing the text with your friends and family members. By helping everyone around you to build their emotional intelligence, you pave the road for more successful interactions in your future.

Thank you and congratulations on your success!

Cognitive Behavioral Therapy

The Definitive Guide to Understanding Your Brain, Depression, Anxiety and How to Overcome It

PUBLISHED BY: (Ryan James)

Copyright © 2017 All rights reserved.

No part of this publication may be copied, reproduced in any format, by any means, electronic or otherwise, without prior consent from the copyright owner and publisher of this book.

Introduction

I want to thank you and congratulate you for downloading Cognitive Behavioral Therapy: The Definitive Guide to Understanding Your Brain, Depression, Anxiety and How to Overcome It.

Depression and anxiety are two very difficult behavioral conditions for patients suffering from their negative effects. They are both difficult to identify and to treat. There are a range of medications and behavioral therapy treatments available, but each method comes with their own challenges, and what might work for one person could prove to be utterly ineffective for another. Compounding the complexity of this issue is the inherent scale on which these problems exist; what could prove to be debilitating for one person is just an inconvenience for another. To share an experience of what depression or anxiety truly feels like is impossible, and often the treatment takes so long to be effective that the sliding scale of improvement makes true analysis of one's progress troublesome.

I decided to write this book to give readers insight into the larger issues surrounding depression and anxiety. I have been suffering with these conditions all my life, and have tried nearly every technique available to try and improve my mental health. Today I live a healthy life, a steady life, but this was not easily obtained. Through all of my treatments, seeing different doctors in separate branches of the medical community, I've come to the realization that there is a first step in combating anxiety and depression, understating. A patient must realize the base root of their anxiety and depression for them to ever get a true handle on how to treat it. This will not make every problem of theirs go away, but it will make the overall process of treatment much easier.

Understanding the mechanics of the human brain in how they relate to anxiety and depression is paramount to being able to improve one's life. This does not need to be a complicated affair, but rather human history needs to be put into perspective of how humans evolved and how mental health conditions came more prominent with advances in technology and ever-progressive social constructs.

Once you have an understanding for how the human brain has come to terms with anxiety and depression in the modern era, you can more effectively treat these mental health concerns. The advice I offer is practical, and comes down to regimenting our bodies in a way similar to our ancestry. It is my hope that by the completion of this book you have a better understanding of what causes anxiety and depression, as well as have a toolbox for how to overcome and treat these illnesses.

If anxiety and depression have proven to be a point of difficulty in your life, then look no further. Keep reading and in a few chapters you will have a better understanding of complex background that affects these conditions; you will have strategies for how to minimize the impact of these mental health concerns, and you will feel confident that you can take your life back into your own hands.

Ryan James

Chapter 1: From Forests to the Urban Sprawl

A Generalized Theory of Anxiety

As our lives become more comfortable, as our standard of living increases, our lives are becoming ever more static. We have routines that take us from our waking hours until we sleep at night. Each day we go through actions that are similar to the day before. There are breaks in this routine, but they are seldom major changes. It may not be the only factor, but a major cause of modern day anxiety is related to the routine of our lives and the static environments in which we spend most of our time.

The first time I heard of theory of static environments being an agitator of anxiety in humans I was skeptical, but over time I have come to appreciate the complexity of this well thought out argument. The basic premise behind the cause of anxiety in modern day humans is that our brains have evolved to be sensitive to minor changes in our environment. This refers to temperature changes over the course of a few days, or a small change like the rattling of a bush in our vision when we are in the woods. The brain has developed to be sensitive to these changes because it was advantageous for human survival. Without being able to notice these changes and act on them, many of our ancestors would have been killed by predators.

In the time since hunter gatherer societies and today, not that much has changed in terms of the human brain. It is still sensitive to the minor changes in our environment, but what happens when those changes simply do not exist? When we spend our days in the same office building, with the same walls and the same equipment and items littered about, we are living in isolation. These environments, while seemingly comfortable for work, can have a devastating effect on the brain if there isn't enough of a break from static. The problem lies with what our brain is expecting versus what it is being fed. Constantly having environments that are static causes the body to go out of balance in terms of when to produce adrenaline. The instinct for fight or flight exists in every person, but the cases of when it is useful has significantly diminished.

The result of our native instincts being placed in our modern environment is that humans often have dramatic reactions to events that do not place us in any real danger. Anxiety goes hand in hand with panic attacks and feelings of helplessness; this is very much the reaction that humans should feel when presented with a life and death situation. The problem is that our modern day events are not life and death; they are solvable problems that simply require a strong will to work through. The fear that one would feels if a large predator suddenly appeared now is invoked in certain individuals when a minor problem arises, such as a large presentation for work. While the presentation itself may be important, it cannot be on the same level of fear as what our ancestors have gone through.

How all of this relates to our anxieties today is simple; our bodies are not used to our modern day qualms and so they produce overreactions to simple problems. While this would be devastating enough, it is not at all the root of our problems. Instead, what many with anxiety suffer from is a result of years of the body becoming acclimated to their environment and producing alarming reactions in the most mundane of events. This is because the human mind is still wired to expect the worst, and so we are constantly on edge.

You may have heard of this idea before. When first presented to me, I was indeed skeptical of how much of this wisdom was relevant in our present day lives. Explaining present day anxiety as it relates to evolution is a satisfying answer, but can it really be correct? I want to stress that there are many factors that create a generalized anxiety disorder, and that this is merely one component to why we feel fear and rushes of adrenaline in the face of minor problems that represent no physical harm. I present this idea first because many of the solutions to treating generalized anxiety come from analyzing this idea and creating situations conducive to how our body expects our environment to be. The tips and advice will come in later chapters, but for now I just wanted to give you a sense of the basis and foundation for how anxiety is analyzed in this book.

A Form of PTSD

In one way or another, every member of modern society is living with some form of Post Traumatic Stress Disorder (PTSD). The first time this idea was presented to me, I thought it alarmist, but as you can see from above, the change in society from forests to cities has created many present day mental health concerns. Humans have not evolved to live in cities, at least not yet. They have not evolved to live static lives that revolve around the same office, the same cafeteria and the same stores. The description of our present day lives would be wholly foreign to our ancestors, and in this comes much of our anxiety.

If you think of modern day anxiety as a form of PTSD, the picture becomes quite clear for what exacerbates this harmful mental state. We are expecting danger, and without an environment that is dynamic and one where we can be on the lookout for predators, our mind has taken to being overactive to minor issues. One must merely take a look at where our anxieties tend to crop up, and put it in perspective of *why* this anxiety is created; you will see that much of our fear is reliant on how our ancestors treated similar situations.

A common cause of my anxiety has been being in social situations where I felt unwelcome. This has nothing to do with whom the actual people were around me, but instead entirely to do with how I *thought* of the people around me. Whether they were coworkers or family, if I felt like a new person to the group my mind would race and I would focus on the minor details of every social engagement. If anxiety is a concern for you, no doubt you have felt the fear and pain of being in a new group. There is concern about saying the right thing, of bringing up the right topic. There is constant anxiety about making a social faux pas. Compounding this issue is that in pleasant society we do not mention to others when they have gone awry, and it is up to the individual to interpret very minor social cues to understand that they have made a mistake. This forces the mind to be ever more vigilant in understanding the actions that one has taken, constantly forcing oneself to analyze their actions and ensure that they have not made a mistake or done something socially unacceptable to the group.

This form of anxiety in the group is a result of our endocrine system being out of sync with our present day lives. It's important to note that there is a fundamental problem, and that our reason for concern is not totally unfounded. It is helpful to be a little bit nervous when in front of a new group, or in front of people in which you are 'unproven'. It instills some fairly important virtues; you are sure to be on your best behavior, and you will be acting to impress and gain acceptance. This is by design, but for those with generalized anxiety, our bodies overact in strong an unpredictable ways. The endocrine system controls the amount of adrenaline released in our body and instead of giving a slight jolt that most others feel, we instead get a large dose that induces panic and causes our severe anxiety.

This is but one form of anxiety, and there are many other cases for how such feelings can manifest. The second and primary method is a worry about the future. Those that suffer with generalized anxiety tend to worry about the future to a greater degree than those not afflicted with the condition. You would think that this would make those with generalized anxiety great planners, but unfortunately fate is not that kind. Instead, what typically happens is the increased level of fear creates a situation of paralysis. A person with anxiety will have a difficult time planning for the future because the chemical reaction in their brain that is supposed to cause a minor amount of worry gets blown out of proportion. In turn the stunned party cannot act and plan for the future. There is too much fear that any one strategy for planning will not be adequate, and so the actions that they take are under constant scrutiny; this scrutiny is self made.

It's incredible that worrying about the future causes so much anxiety in the present, but unfortunately anxiety is a condition that makes us fearful of the future and stunts our ability to act in the present. The constant worry about the future manifests in being wholly unprepared for the present. Though there is thought about the future, the present offers a situation where our brain takes in current events and puts them in the perspective of the future that we are worried about. This is a slightly more complicated idea, but imagine this example: you are at a holiday office party. You know most of your coworkers there but a boss is flying in from out of town. This is your boss's boss, and making a good impression with him or her will have long lasting consequences on how you will move up in the company. The worry about what this social meeting will mean for the future forces the mind to overanalyze the present. Each action that is taken around the boss that you've never met before is magnified. This is made worse because the good actions are never taken with the same amount of significance as the actions that you are worried will make a poor impression. This is a result of looking to the future. By worrying what will come in the future, you are taking the present day events and always creating a worst case scenario for what could happen. No action that you take, even making a good impression, will create a long lasting picture of the future where you are successful. Instead, the mind constantly wanders to picturing how any of your present day actions will cause harm to you or your career in the future.

This status quo of planning for the worst may not seem fair, but again its origins lie in evolution. You just saw an example of how no matter what action is taken at a holiday party, a worker with anxiety will put it in the perspective of a negative action that will affect their future. Imagine now a farmer from centuries ago, far removed from hunter-gatherer society, but not living in our fast paced present. The worry of the future is a net benefit to the farmer; they are able to plan around the seasons and produce a reasonable calendar for harvest. The key difference that I want you to focus on is the possible outcomes for the farmer versus the office worker. The farmer can expect that either the harvest will be good or will be bad. They can almost certainly expect some amount of product from their efforts, and understand the worst case and best case scenarios. The number of outcomes is ultimately fairly limited, and so their fears are put into a perspective that they can plainly see. Our office worker does not have this luxury. They are instead presented with limitless outcomes for what their future in the company will be. Granted it ultimately comes down to whether or not they stay at the company, but how they stay at the company or are forced out come with many different outcomes. The not knowing about the possible outcomes for our office worker is what presents them with a greater level of fear and anxiety than the farmer.

There is a second component beyond outcomes that leaves the farmer in a better position than the office worker. The actions that the farmer takes towards producing a good harvest are ultimately fairly simple. They know what actions to take to produce a good outcome for themself. The office worker does not have it as easy. What will produce the best outcome is a complex set of social interactions and outputted work. It is in no way clear what they need to accomplish in the next six months to have the best possible outcome. This ensures that the fear they have about their future is not in their control.

In essence, this is the anxiety that we feel today. It is a worry of the uncertain future coupled with our inability to know how our present day actions will affect that future. This is a factor of so much of our lives being determined by social hierarchy and social cues. It is much harder to determine the outcomes of social interactions than it is to determine the outcome of the work that a farmer does. For one, the outcomes are limitless and any small action could dictate the future of the office worker. The farmer has a much more narrow set of outcomes, and the work they do can be see in the context of the harvest much more clearly. This is the most common form of our anxiety, and is the base root of our anxiety. Chapters four through six will offer strategies for dealing with this type of anxiety, but before moving on, there is one additional aspect of modern day anxiety I want to focus on; how technology has exacerbated the problems presented by society and our change from nature to the cities.

Information Overload

Static environments, concerns of the future and how our actions determine our future are just some of the factors that contribute to anxiety. In the age of information there is another component that cannot be ignored, the constant flow of information that surrounds us at all times. From the phones in our pockets, to our ever increasing flow of emails, to the constant comparing of one another through social media, technology has improved the ease of our lives at nearly the same rate that it has increased our anxieties.

We are bombarded with information left and right from our waking hours until we sleep at night. There isn't a period greater than sixty seconds where we don't take out our cell phone and look at the trending headlines. We are presented with more information today than at any period in history. While this has been fantastic for learning and creating a more aware society, it has brought with it the problems of too much information. We don't have peaceful moments the way our ancestors did, and without these moments of downtime and total cease of new information, it proves to be too much for our brains. This is half of the information overload problem; our constant reliance on technology to feel connected to the world. It's not about the news stories that we read or the events happening in the world. The problem arises from feeling left out when we are not participating and gaining knowledge and insight into world events. There is a sense of anxiety for some in simply not knowing what the rest of the world is doing. You may have felt this before, a sense that you are missing out by simply not being connected to your phone throughout the day. This is a feeling that persists for many and is the result of training yourself to be constantly occupied and connected through your smart phone.

The second half of anxiety due to technology comes in our constant comparison of one another. This idea will come up with depression, and is more central to that mental health condition, but it is relevant to anxiety as well. By comparing ourselves to our peers, we bring additional stress and worry. Suddenly it is not just our fear about our own lives and where our future is heading, but now we have an unrealistic benchmark to compare ourselves to. Remember that what you see on social media doesn't represent the true lives of our peers. They are instead just snapshots of the high points of their lives. Looking at these high points, it is impossible to compare our ordinary days to the best days that our friends will experience. It produces the feeling that we are both missing out, and that we are slow in accomplishing our dreams. It produces anxiety that we must achieve more, and that we must do it quickly.

Summary

Generalized anxiety disorder is a complicated mental health condition that has numerous factors. It is impossible to discern each and every factor, in particular how they relate to the individual. No two people share the same anxieties, nor are those anxieties of the same magnitude. To get a better hold of anxiety, and to understand how it manifests, one must merely put into perspective our modern lives and how they compare to the lives of hunter-gatherers, as well as farmers. By understanding the slower points in human life, we can see how our bodies have been trained for different conditions than the society that we currently live in. Understanding where our anxieties come from, if only partially, is crucial for understanding how to reduce anxieties' impact on our lives.

Chapter 2: Understanding Depression

A Well Known Enigma

Depression is one of the most common mental illnesses in the world. In the United States alone, there are some fifteen million adults that have been diagnosed with depression. While this number is large, the true number of adults afflicted with depression is likely significantly larger. Depression is a mental disorder that, even for its popularity, is still poorly understood. It is known to be caused by a multitude of factors, some genetic and some lifestyle. Treatment options that are available are immense, and while there are some treatments that are more proven than others, there is no single cure all for depression.

I was diagnosed with depression when I was in college. My diagnosis, like many, was a bittersweet moment. It was nice to put a label on a debilitating aspect of my life and to find treatment, but at the same time the title of depression brings with it a stigma and burden of being classified. Knowing that you have clinical depression means that you are accepting your label and are open to treatment. This is a necessary step for those with depression, but there is an initial period of worry about merely having the label by itself; it is seen sometimes as a character flaw, particularly by the individual with the diagnosis. This is an unfortunate side effect of how society has treated depression over the years. Unlike conditions such as Bipolar disorder, the term 'depression' has many outside uses. These uses have helped color the word over time, and patients see depression as far more than a mental illness. They see it at as something that perhaps they can avoid. They see it as something that everyone goes through, and that it possibly doesn't warrant getting help from a medical professional.

While attitudes on this are changing, I want to point out that if you are suffering from depression, you shouldn't feel ashamed. You should try and distance the term 'depression' from the condition of depression. One is a term that has been used for centuries and has taken on a negative connotation that is exercisable by all. The medical term is by far very different, and is something that not everyone experiences. Depression is a lifelong mental disorder and one that needs persistent treatment if it is to be curbed significantly.

Primary Factors

While there are many causes for depression, for the purposes of this book I want to focus on two primary factors: time and comparison. Depression is hard to separate from anxiety, and often a patient will experience both instead of just a single one of these conditions. It should be no surprise that those suffering with depression have difficulty living in the moment; this is exactly the same as those that suffer from generalized anxiety disorder. While those with anxiety tend to focus on the future, patients with depression tend to linger in the past. This focus on their history and their past actions causes the suffering of how they perceive the present and their future. The past consumes their time and so the present becomes a period that is difficult to contemplate. The future becomes almost wholly irrelevant, as a patient will focus so much on the past that they cannot dare plan about their future.

The later chapters have many tips that deal with this first factor of depression, time. If you or a loved one suffer from depression, it should be a major goal to put into perspective the past and to start living in the current moment. You've no doubt noticed that those with depression linger on the past, but it's almost important to note *how* they view the past. Depression is like a lens covered in dust. It takes all moments, good and bad, and makes them murky. It takes moments from the past and adds an air of misery and sadness to events. How often have you thought of your past and put that event in the perspective of what you did wrong? This is something that everyone experiences, but for those with depression, they tend to view all events through this difficult lens. They see all actions that they've done as deciding factors for how they currently feel. This is a difficult condition to treat, and one of the things that can help is reframing the past. We cannot change our past actions, but we can certainly change how we put them into perspective. By looking at our actions and the actions of others that have caused sorrow in the present, we can try and reduce that sadness by softening the overall impact of those actions. The moment that an individual starts to live in the present, and not just the past, is when they start to feel better about themselves. Focusing on the present means that one cannot wallow about the past.

    The second major component to depression is in comparison. This too is very similar as to why anxiety can be exacerbated. Depression has always grown stronger when a person with depression compares themselves to their peers. This constant fight within the mind to prove yourself relative to others causes sadness. In our present day it is easier than ever for people to compare themselves to others. Often this comparison is done because of social media. When we read a tweet about our friend's vacation, or when we see their Facebook photos, we can't help but compare our present day situation to the high points of their life. Granted the photos our friend posts do not contain the low points of their trip. It doesn't contain when the kids were complaining on the car ride; it doesn't show the fight a husband got in with his wife. For those with depression, this doesn't matter. They see the high points in the life of their friends and they can only compare how they are feeling to how their friend appears to be feeling in the photos they post online. Even if you don't suffer from major depressive disorder, it is highly likely that you feel a tinge of sadness when you compare yourself to your friend's Facebook feed. This is completely normal and should be expected, but for those with depression this feeling lingers for a much longer period of time. In accordance with treating depression by growing to live in the moment, one needs to separate themselves from their peers. They should be social with their peers, but should not constantly try and compare themselves. You must remember that those with depression do not treat themselves fairly and will always compare themselves in a less than favorable way. The best way to begin the avoidance of this problem is by stopping comparison whenever possible; this is why I strongly advocate removing Facebook if you suffer from depression.

Time and comparison; these are just two factors that I focus on, but know that there are many more. Depression is not just from conditioning, but has shown to be hereditary. The exact percentage of contribution from each factor is unknown, but the treatment is going to be the same regardless of *why* an individual suffers from depression. To treat depression is to embark on a life long battle. It is a fight that you must be vigilante in, but one that can be won with routine, a routine that enforces positive feelings and the value of self worth.

Drug Use and Depression

I have worked with many that suffer from depression. In my time, I have noticed a high correlation between drug use and depression. What came first does not matter, and I don't want to comment on how drug use may cause depression, but rather want to focus on the outcome of using drugs when depressed. Depression has many causes, but the exact mechanical cause in the brain comes down to a chemical imbalance. How this is treated is going to be the same regardless of how this chemical imbalance came to be. That being said, I want to stress that if an individual has been using narcotics to treat their depression, it is a harder road to find stability and happiness. This is because of how drugs affect the brain in the long run, further distorting the chemical imbalance in the brain. I mention this because if you or a loved one use narcotics and suffer from depression, it is paramount to treat a drug addition to also treat depression. You cannot solve one issue without solving the other issue. In addition, understand that it takes longer for those that have abused narcotics to feel good about themselves, the longer it will take to reduce the symptoms of depression. This is not meant to instill a sense of worry in those that have abused narcotics, but I have found that explaining the uphill battle that awaits readies patients for the road ahead. I have seen many that have abused narcotics and overcome their depression, in addition to their drug habit. It can be done, but that individual must prepare themselves and be ready to treat both conditions simultaneously.

Soft Bipolar

Bipolar disorder is a common mental illness. Traditionally there have been two forms of bipolar disorder, identified as Bipolar I and Bipolar II. Bipolar I is categorized as having period of being manic with period of being depressed. Bipolar II however is much similar to depression. It is categorized as having period of hypomania, a light form of mania, with period of extreme depression. In recent times, as of the DSM-V (Diagnostic and Statistics Manual of Mental Disorders, 5th Edition), Bipolar disorder is now thought of as being on a spectrum. There is still a measure of Bipolar I and II, but it is accepted there is a far larger range of how Bipolar affects different people. I mention this here because of the rising idea of 'soft' bipolar. Soft bipolar is extremely similar to depression, so much so that many that have be diagnosed with depression may instead have soft bipolar. The distinction is important because the treatment is quite different. While there are many measures that someone with depression can take to treat their depression, it is much more difficult to treat bipolar disorder without medication.

Soft Bipolar looks so similar to depression because the primary characteristics of the disorder are nearly identical to depression. Soft Bipolar is characterized as by having period of extreme depression mixed with period of 'normal', or a time when depressive characteristics are not as pronounced. This book does not aim to treat or even offer advice for treating soft bipolar, but I realize that readers of this book might suffer from depression. If you believe that the alternating between depressive states and some level of normalcy better describes you than major depressive disorder, I suggest you consult with your doctor. I insert this here merely to bring this disorder to your attention, as it is still fairly new and not well known.

Chapter 3: The Intersection of Anxiety and Depression

The advice in this book is meant to be a practical guide for treating both depression and anxiety. Chapter one and two have helped establish general theories on both disorders, but as you can see they are heavily intertwined. There is more than a strong correlation between the number of people that suffer from depression and anxiety. More importantly, how they suffer is quite similar; both stemming from comparing oneself to others and difficulty in farming the present with the future and the past.

As you continue into the later chapters I want to make very clear that all of the advice in this book is based on my own experiences. That is to say, the advice of the various doctors that I have had over the years, built upon my own experiences and research that I have done. Each method of solving for anxiety and depression have been proven to work, but the degree of effectiveness is highly variable. You may find that a single method is highly effective, or you may find that you need to combine several different methods to reduce your anxiety and depression. It's going to be different for everyone, but it is essential that you never give up. You must stick to a healthy routine to feel better about yourself. Do not waver in your fight against depression and anxiety. Stick to the tips in this book and you will be in a better place than where you started.

Lastly, sticking to a routine when you suffer from depression is very difficult. The mental disorder is categorized by difficulty in finding motivation to participate in life, and ironically this is very much the thing you must do to make yourself feel better. You must make strives to take action before you feel improvement, knowing that improvement in how you feel is a matter of doing these actions first and feeling the result later.

Chapter 4: Things You Can Do Today

Sleep

You know a good night's sleep is important – you've been hearing this all of your life. What you might not know is that sleep is an essential part of combating social anxiety and depression. Poor sleep leads to a body that is unbalanced on a fundamental level. Your adrenaline levels are completely out of sync and your body uses too much effort on activities that should not be stress inducing. You are unable to use your body's energy on the things that matter most, instead wasting your body's energy on negative thoughts that create your anxiety.

So how do we get a good night's sleep? Unfortunately it is easier said than done, and in our ever increasingly technology driven lives, this is only getting more difficult. You will need to create a regimen for yourself, and be diligent – this is something that you will need to follow everyday to see the best results. About an hour or two before bedtime, start preparing for bed. This doesn't mean brushing your teeth at eight at night, but rather you must simply stop working and only engage in relaxing activities. These activities can include watching a movie or listening to music, but you mustn't exercise, answer emails, or spend your evening hours arguing on online forums. About thirty minutes before bedtime you are going to want to cut off all screen time. This means turning off the television, your computer, and your cell phone. This last part is a little bit difficult for some people as our phones have become an essential part of our lives, but that is why we must plan a regimen and know that at thirty minutes before bed, we shut our phone down or agree to not look at the screen and to put all notifications on silent. It's a little effort at first, but chances are the quality of your sleep is not as good as it otherwise could be. Try these tips and it'll be worth the effort for that feeling of waking up relaxed and ready for the day. You'll find your sleep has improved your anxiety through rebalancing your energy levels and reducing your natural stress levels through the release of cortisone in your sleep.

Praise the Sun

You don't need to actually *praise* the sun per-say, but you do need to appreciate its glow. This means going outside and basking in the warm embrace of our star. You need to do this because a deficiency in vitamin D leads to increased levels of stress and anxiety, causing negative feelings. Getting into nature and embracing the warm sun lets our body soak up this beneficial vitamin. Time in the sun has also shown to improve cognitive function and to reduce the levels of depression in many patients.

There is no reason not to follow this easy tip. Some portion of your non-working day involves staring at your phone, reading, or using a portable computer. Take this opportunity to do this activity outside. Your time in the sun does not need to be a sweat inducing event – you simply need to put in the time and enjoy some of the sun's rays, even passively. All it takes is thirty minutes a day and within two to three weeks you should be feeling better and having less anxiety at social events.

Music

I thought it was just me, until I realized that this is common amongst all my friends. After high school and college, so many of us stop listening to music, or do so with far less frequency. We also tend to just listen to what is available, like on the radio or a streaming service. We do not seek out our favorite songs and listen to them repeatedly over the span of several months. Why do we stop doing this? For me personally it was simply a matter of practicality and the number of hours in the day, but listening to music is a simple activity to add into your life that will show benefits for years to come.

Find the music that you enjoy listening to and find a way to obtain that music. You will want to be able to listen to the same few songs whenever you want. This music does not all need to be pop and happy – just listen to the music that you like and what makes you feel good. If you are able to listen to music in a situation that make you nervous, put on that song that you have been hearing for a few months and notice how much better you feel. The thoughts in your head will fade out as memories of activities done while listening to the music will come rushing to mind. You have probably had this experience before – listening to a song and having it take you back to the place and time that you associate with the melody. You want this effect. Music can be like a time machine for your mind and your emotions. Listening to the right song at the wrong time can make all the difference in the world. Try this tip, and even I you can't listen to music in public, you can still enjoy the stress reducing benefits of listening to music on your way home from work or while relaxing before bed.

Arriving on Time

We tend to only remember anxiety as it strikes us in a public place. Whether this is a supermarket trip, a job interview, or meeting a date, we remember the places and associate them with our anxiety because that is when it is at its peak. The truth is that our anxiety starts much before we ever get to the public venue. It usually starts with how we are feeling on the way to our event. People with strong social anxiety tend to be late for events because of their time spent worrying, their time spent thinking through the situation they are about to encounter. What many fail to realize is that the resulting lateness is a key promoter of the stress and anxiety we feel when around other people. Even if it does not matter to the event host that you are late, your mind will still focus on the clock as you are approaching and provide negative thoughts before you ever even enter the social situation.

We can solve this problem by just providing ten or fifteen extra minutes for travel time. This is a very easy solution, but in practice is extremely difficult to implement. We grow into our routines if you are routinely late for events, or simply do not plan enough travel time, adding an extra ten or fifteen minutes is going to be a challenge. The key is to remind yourself that you need this extra time and that this small change will have a large impact on how you feel during a social event. Having the extra time allows us to arrive at a location early, preparing ourselves before we have to go inside and face our company. Remind yourself frequently about the importance of travel time and you will make it a necessary part of your life.

Cleanliness

After a long and stressful day, nothing is worse than coming home to a disorganized mess. This doesn't mean a display like something from *Hoarders*, but rather just a home where you have difficulty finding things, or a place that you would feel uncomfortable showing other people without tidying up first. The feeling of a disorganized home is something that you take with you wherever you go. Our home is part of our identity, and a fundamental part of social anxiety is a worry about who we are. By cleaning our home and making it ready to present to guests, we feel better about ourselves and who we are. We are taking a physical representation of ourselves and giving it the best possible angle at how it looks. In addition, not being able to find what you are looking for is a key part of how anxiety builds in our body. If this is a common occurrence then the buildup can spillover into social situations and make us feel wholly uncomfortable. You must keep a clean home, and with that you will feel better about yourself and not get frustrated by not being able to find items when you need them.

Cleaning is difficult and none of us want to do it, but know the benefits that a clean home brings and you will be more motivated to make your home a comfortable place for you to live, and one where you would love to have guests over and show them around. A tip for how to get started is by taking a survey of your living room, kitchen, and bedroom. This is probably where you spend most of your time and will be the key parts to making your home clean and a relaxing place to spend your time. Do not try and clean your entire home in a single day. Instead, focus on a single room at a time. Breaking down what you need to accomplish into smaller steps is a surefire way to create a feeling of accomplishment. Work on this for a few weeks, or up to a month, and expect to see improved results about how you feel almost immediately. Being able to find what you need when you need it reduces much of the stress created when searching for something frantically right before you need to leave to engage in a social situation. Also, by simply being around your clean home you will feel miles better about yourself. You can take this feeling and bring it out with you into the world and curb your stress.

Frame Your Problems

Not knowing what future events will hold is a leading cause of our anxiety and depression. We can cut down on this feeling by simply making a list of the tasks that we need to accomplish and think about them one by one. This serves a couple of purposes. For one, it helps organize your thoughts into individual pieces. You wont' think about your 'big project' as just a large singular task to accomplish, you will instead think about it as the component parts that you know how to tackle. Breaking down larger tasks in this way makes them less threatening and reinvigorates you to tackle the task. Two, looking at all of the things you need to accomplish frees your mind from having to juggle all of your future tasks. Your mind is partially stressed because it is juggling your calendar and thinking about all of your upcoming events, and also consistently searching for tasks that may have been forgotten as well. It's a simple trick, but the organization of knowing what you need to accomplish really does improve how you think about your tasks at hand. Once you can look at your work as solvable problems, then you will be motivated to take on the tasks and feel less stressed in other situations where you mind wanders to work.

To get started with making to-do lists, start with organizing the simple parts of your life. I suggest starting with a supermarket list and organizing all of the food and items you need. It's a simple start, but you'll notice that if you used to stress mid week about food shopping, that having a list of what is needed helps cut down on this thought process, freeing your mind to focus on other tasks or simply appreciate your free time. You can quickly move on from simple lists about organizing your home to more complicated lists about your work, or even future life goals. Organize the work that needs to be done by your company and break down each task as an easy, medium, or difficult challenge. This helps be realistic about the list and puts into perspective that not every task is identical in difficulty. Work on a set task and return to your checklist to cross off the completed item. This simple action brings a feeling of achievement as you've reached a milestone and know that part of your larger project is complete.

For large goals, goals that can take place in ten or twenty years, make sure that you break these down into extremely granular pieces. Looking at where you want to be in ten years and where you are now can be a real challenge. It can seem like there is no set process you can take to get to where you want to be, but by breaking down the tasks that you need to accomplish you can both be realistic about future goals, and you can organize the small moves you need to make everyday to get to the person that you want to be. Organize your life and start by breaking down simple tasks, and then move onto larger projects and map out all you need to accomplish. Keep that list and cross off completed tasks. If you are ever feeling stressed or worried about upcoming events, simply look at your checklist and note the marked off items. You've started this task, you've worked through some of it already. This thought should ease your tension and help with your anxiety around your coworkers at the office.

Solve One Problem of Yours

If a panic attack feels like it's coming on at work there is a small simple trick you can do to rid this feeling, or at least put it off temporarily. Your anxiety at work comes partially from a fear of failure. You are worried that you might not be able to complete the task at hand, or that when it is turned in your superiors will find the work unacceptable. Even if this is not being processed in your conscious mind, the thought is still buried deep in the depths of your anxiety. You need a way to know that you are capable of solving this project. You need something that can quickly build your confidence and show yourself that you are the right person for the job. This activity also needs to be fun and engaging enough that we can move our mind from worrying to having fun. The best way to solve this larger problem is by solving a simple problem, preferably in the form of a game or puzzle.

Perhaps you already play something like Sudoku, and if you do that's great - you already have a tool at your disposal.

The next step is taking this fun distraction and using it when you feel a great burden on your shoulder. If you don't already have a game, I suggest a mentally challenging but complete-able puzzle, something like a Crossword or game of Minesweeper. Games like Tetris and Candy Crush are certainly engaging, but the milestones area a little harder to separate. In Candy Crush much of the progress comes from a randomly generated level that you have no control over – you may just progress out of luck, or get stuck due to randomness. Tetris has a similar problem but is made worse because the game simply isn't that mentally taxing. It has more to do with coordination and we want to find a sense of mental accomplishment. Take your puzzle and complete a few steps of it. This means filling in a few Crossword clues or working part of the way through a Sudoku. Look at the puzzle that you have finished and embrace the feeling of accomplishment. It's a small achievement, but you've shown that you have the mental strength and fortitude to complete a challenging mental task. Now your mind should be ready to take on more challenges as it refocuses on the now and away for the upcoming work that was causing your anxiety and stress at work.

Chapter 5: Things You Can Do Tomorrow

Overload Your Own Senses

The feeling of watching eyes, of thoughts in the room focused on you; the notion that somehow you don't fit in with the room you're in. All of this is caused by an overactive nervous system and an adrenal gland that is not properly separating life and death situations from large rooms with new or uncomfortable groups of people. There are many ways to find short term relief from this effect, but by and far my favorite is with a quick shock to your sense. I recommend this tip only because I tried it, and I was shocked about how effective it was. The goal here is you want to send a surge of real adrenaline to your body, adrenaline caused by the fear of dying. When put back into normal non life threatening events, the feelings of social anxiety and stress are much less pronounced. You will feel more at ease purely because your mind is able to separate out the events that truly require your body's energy, versus the events that you are overreacting to.

There are several ways of sending a shock of adrenaline to your system, but the trick that worked for me was skydiving. This might sound a bit scary, but that is exactly the point of the practice. Skydiving is actually incredibly safe with virtually no fatalities in any given year, but the effect on your brain of jumping out of plane will stay with you for long after the jump. Jump sites can be found outside of most cities, and rates for skydiving are quite reasonable, usually a few hundred dollars a jump. You do not need months of training as a simple course on the day of the jump is all that is required in terms of knowledge. If you decide to go this route, know that you won't be jumping alone, or at least not on your first jump. An instructor will be tethered to you and you will be using his or her parachute to land. You do no need to worry about pulling a lever or making sure your harness is on correctly – the teacher will take care of all of these aspects. All you need to do is fly to Earth, send a shock to your system, and then reap the benefits of reduced stress the next time you are in a social situation.

Skydiving for many people is going to be an immediate turn off. You might have a fear of flying or heights, or you may not have the means to go skydiving at all. There are other ways of pumping your adrenal glands and surging your body with energy. It will take longer but you can do this through exercise, and this is generally recommended for treating all types of anxieties as well. You can also try slightly less shocking events like riding a rollercoaster or a fast moving amusement park ride. You want to give yourself the feeling of a racing heart brought on by something other than social anxiety. Replicating this feeling in other situations reduces the severity of panic when you are in a social environment.

Exercise

It's a simple tip but it certainly isn't easy. Exercise is hard work but it's also been proven to be one of the most, if not flat out the most, effective methods in treating social anxiety and depression. The goal of exercise is to even your body's energy distribution throughout the day, raise your metabolism, and produce endorphins through the build up of muscle. There is no downside to exercise, although it does take time, potentially some equipment, and a location to exercise. To get the best results you will want to focus on both cardio and weight lifting. There is a positive correlation in both those that run more, and those that increase muscle mass, and a decrease in their levels of generalized anxiety. This extends to all types of fitness and exercise, and at a very minimum, your improved body will make you feel better about your self and enhance your body image.

To get started you will first want to create a schedule. It's a step a lot of people overlook, but it's an essential part of ensuring that you exercise consistently and are realistic about your muscle and weight goals. Try and just focus on three times a week. Plan it around days that you know are free, and do not plan on waking up earlier or staying up later to exercise. You want to work your exercise into your existing schedule. Try and find a fun activity to participate in and this will improve your chances of sticking to an exercise plan. This might include joining a local soccer team, or meeting some friends for a game of Frisbee. You are likely nervous about joining another group due to anxiety, and so remember that a gym, or even your own home, are perfectly suitable substitutes.

For a cardio workout, I recommend getting twenty to thirty minutes of heavy breathing and an increase in your core body temperature. We are working out purely to sweat when it comes to cardio. You want to get your heart rate high and maintain that level for fifteen to twenty minutes. This increased heart level will translate to a more relaxed heart when in difficult social situations. Your enhanced cardiovascular system will significantly reduce the physical effects you feel from stress. This includes things like sweating or getting red in the face and extremities. If you aren't in condition to go running, or get your heart beat appropriately high, that's perfectly fine. Start with walking and work your way up from there. Even if you never move past walking you will still be at a significant advantage to where you were before. The effects will be less pronounced, but you should notice a decrease in all physical symptoms brought on from social anxiety.

Weight lifting is slightly easier proposition, but it is

needed in conjunction with a good cardio workout. Weightlifting will tear the muscle fibers in your body, replacing them with stronger fibers and making you more buff and create a lean desirable definition. The real benefit comes in our brain's response to weight lifting where endorphins flow because we are gaining muscle. The endorphins sent out improve our mood and reduce our stress. This effect is long lasting and will carry itself to your workplace. There are many different weight lifting techniques, but you should be doing them about ten minutes of lifting three to four times a week. You can do these on the same days as your cardio workout, or you can do them on separate days. If you do not have the proper equipment for weight lifting, that is no problem. Simply use your body's existing weight and focus on exercises like crunches, sit-ups, and pushups. It's a small time investment for a long lasting benefit that will make you feel better about yourself and improve your self-image to ease your anxiety during social situations.

Feel Great from a Great Diet

A fundamental change to your diet is required if you want to rid yourself of depression and anxiety. It's a long form step and will take many months to see the true benefits of changing one's diet, but don't fret, there is one step that you can do today to alleviate some of the stress you might currently have.

Food is an essential part of our culture and our history. When feeling down or depressed after a long day, or even when out at a social function where food is being served, one of the best things we can do is simply eat a good comfort food. Comfort food is going to be different for every individual and be even more different across cultures. Take a moment to enjoy a meal that you truly love, something that remind you of home and brings on feelings of love and care. For me personally, that means eating a good meatloaf dinner with mashed potatoes, peas, and gravy. It's not a health conscious move, that's for sure, but that doesn't make me feel any less better when I'm done eating. The aim in comfort foods is not for nutrition or health, but rather just to get a sense of the safety and security that we felt when we were younger. Even if right now isn't a time that you need to munch on a security food, you should still map out the restaurants and grocery stores around you where you can find some comfort food. Think about what food your family used to eat when you were younger and try and bring this feeling back to life. Don't worry about the cost too much either – this isn't something you should be doing very often. There is a chance that comfort food makes you feel worse, it just remind you of home and brings you deeper into a stupor, and in this case you already know that you should avoid comfort food. If this describes you, or even if you find success with comfort food, there is another aspect of our health identified with food, and that's our general diet.

    A dietary shift is hard, especially if we are moving from a mostly innutritious diet to a healthy nutritious one. Comfort food aside, so much of the food that is boxed or frozen is loaded with salt, fats, and needless preservatives. This gunk might make you feel better in the short term, but in the long term it weakens your immune system, causes weight gain, and can leave you feeling out of energy and tired just shortly after completing a meal. You instead need to focus on nutritious healthy foods that will leave you feeling energized and fresh. To change your diet on such a basic level, you're going to need to make some hard changes. For one, identify your current diet and figure out the trouble spots. There are invariably some meals that you have that have little to no nutritional value. We want to axe these in favor of more nutritious and fresh foods. Find a simple cookbook and work with the recipes within to find the foods that you like and are easy to make. We live in a time where many cookbooks cater to those that have limited time and are not necessarily knowledgeable about the various vegetables and spices we need. These books have easy recipes that can frequently be completed in less than thirty minutes. Use this as a guide and mix it with other recipes of foods from different regions. The recipes are important, but they are only as helpful as the quality of the ingredients.

A change to a healthier diet does not need to be an expensive shift. When people think of quality ingredients they think of the expensive organic foods at their local supermarket. I want you to know that you do not need to eat organic to eat healthy. Organic foods commonly carry just as many pesticides as foods that are not labeled organic. Focus on the quality of the fruits and vegetables you buy based on look and feel, and never worry about the label. For meats, poultry and fish, buy from your local butcher at your supermarket. Never buy the precut meats as these are never as good as the ones cut right in front of you. Your butcher has to see your face when he hands you your product – this just isn't the case with those that are selling you meats that are prepackaged. Once you have the foods you are going to prepare and the recipes you are going to use, you can start to focus on the joy of cooking.

There is something essential, Earthly even, to cooking. There is a strong connection between what you are putting in your body and how you feel. Knowing that the food in your stomach was selected and prepared by you will have an immediate positive effect. You can literally see these benefits within two to three days. At work or at a social situation you will feel better as you know that your body is filled with foods that it needs, and not unwanted and unnecessary chemicals and preservatives. There is also simply the act of cooking itself. It is a relaxing experience in the evening and you can melt away the day's stresses by preparing your food and embracing the feelings and sensations that come from cutting, dicing, and washing your food. Eating comfort food is an absolutely great way to feel better immediately, but refining your diet over time will have life long benefits affecting everything from health to the way you feel around others.

Chapter 6: Looking to Your Future

Consider Finding a Professional to Talk To

Communication and therapy can be a vital part to improving your anxiety and depression. This is a step that many sufferers of these disorders simply to not wish to partake in. Finding a therapist should not be a scary situation, but you should know that it is time consuming and could potentially be cost prohibitive. Provided you have the option, pure therapy is recommended before turning to medications. The advantage of a therapist is that they help delve into your underlying problems. You might find that your social anxiety is simply a point on part of spectrum of a larger problem. I myself have never found a therapist that I truly liked, however I have had friends that found wonderful therapists and that helped them through all sort of difficulties in their lives. I see the potential benefit to a therapist as a huge plus, but the first few steps that you have to take to finding one are harder than they need to be.

If you've decided that you'd like to find a therapist, your first step is going to be looking at your finances and your health insurance plan. As part of the Obama-Care act of 2012, mental health services are a required feature of all plans that are featured on the exchange. This almost always means that you have an option to find a therapist and go to a few appointments and your insurance company will cover the cost. There are many therapists that operate out of network and will not be covered on any insurance policy. You can expect these therapists to have a stronger pedigree than many that would be covered by insurance, and you can also expect that they cost a decent chunk of change more. From my experience of searching, I found that sessions could range anywhere from $200 to $500, and that a session was typically defined as somewhere between thirty minutes and an hour. This is quite the price to pay, but depending on your financial situation you may find that these top tier of therapists are right for you. If your finances dictate that you cannot see someone that charges so much, you have no reason to fear, a large part of the therapy process is simply talking through your problems, and it doesn't matter so much who is on the other side receiving the information. To find a more moderately priced therapist, go to your healthcare provider's website and do a doctor lookup for 'behavioral care'. Part of the reason that many people do not move beyond this step is because there is no lookup for a 'therapist' – the name will always be listed as 'behavioral care' or some other similar description. Make sure that you find doctors that are not listed as psychiatrists. A psychiatrist will always turn to prescription medicine to aid in solving a problem, whereas a therapist will always talk the problem through with you. Once you have found a doctor near you, check with your insurance policy to see what your co pay for secessions will be, as well as how many secessions you have before you have to pay out of pocket. When I first started looking for therapist, I was surprised to find that my health insurance would only pay for ten appointments, and any session after this would be hundreds of dollars. If your insurance policy looks something similar to the way that mine did, then I suggest that you look to a different method of therapy. You will have to rely on your friends and family to speak through your problems, but don't worry, there are steps for that situation as well.

    You will know that you have found a good person to talk to when they can just sit and listen, and all of this without you feeling as though they are being judgmental. It's important to share your experiences with others – this is one of the key advantages of finding a significant other. The advice that they give is not as important as the fact that they are understanding of your personal struggle. You want to make sure that every word that you say to them is being registered and that they do not zone out, or give you the feeling they are not paying attention. Knowing that another person is listening to your problems brings a sense of unity with others, a sense that your struggles are not unique, but in fact something that we all deal with, simply on a different scale. Finding someone to talk to is scary – you are sharing your life experiences with this person and asking for advice on very personal situations, but follow the steps above and you will find someone that can help you and make you feel less anxious in crowds.

Consider Medication

It's a discussion that you must ultimately have with your doctor, but depending on how long you've lived with your depression and anxiety, it might be time to look at medications. I want to give you a brief overview of some of your options in case you decide to talk to a doctor. I myself have two medications, one that I take daily for depression and one that I *can* take for anxiety. I have found the other tips in this book to be enough of a booster that I don't need my anti-anxiety medication, but if things got truly unbearable I could take it, and from past experiences I know that it truly does work.

You must keep in mind that treating anxiety with medication is unlike treating other mental ailments. Usually there is something coupled with social anxiety, like depression or a generalized anxiety disorder. In cases of a persistent model of irregular thought processes, a doctor will likely recommend an anti-depressant. Antidepressants do more than just treat depression; they can ease your anxiety over time. The range in price, side effects and primary effects of antidepressants is wide and varied. If you feel like social anxiety is your sole issue, I would not recommend taking stronger, more expensive non-generic antidepressants. The side effects and price probably aren't worth the possible benefits. For most suffering from depression, common antidepressants that have been on the market for years tend to be highly effective. They are proven drugs that are among the safest on the market, due to their extensive testing and begin in use for decades.

For treating rapid onset anxiety, there are a few drugs that are commonly prescribed. Not quite as common as antidepressants, Xanax or the generic equivalent works to relieve all types of anxiety very quickly. This is the drug that I have access to but rarely ever take. As I said I found success with these other tips and have not needed to rely on this powerful relaxer, however it is just that, it does relax and it is extremely powerful. I would describe it as having one to three alcoholic drinks, depending on dosage, in rapid succession. The feeling is slightly different than alcohol in that you are a little bit more alert and you won't be slurring your speech, unless at very high doses. The main problem with these types of drugs, Xanax or others in the benzodiazepine family, is that they are habit forming, lose effectiveness over time, and will almost never be prescribed for daily intake for a period longer than thirty days. If your anxiety is truly life debilitating, there is a chance that your doctor will recommend taking Xanax everyday, but even in these cases such a treatment plan does not exceed thirty days. The reason is that all of these types of rapid acting drugs are extremely addictive, both physically and mentally. Taking them for long period of time can also cause a variety of respiratory problems and other health issues.

I hope that you are able to use the other tips in this book to resolve your anxiety and depression, but if you do take the medication route, it's important to weigh your options. Think through what a treatment means and whether or not you want your anxiety to be dependent on a drug. Most importantly, if you do decide to take drugs, speak with your doctor and work through an appropriate regimen that fits you.

Conclusion

Thank you again for downloading *Cognitive Behavioral Therapy: The Definitive Guide to Understanding Your Brain, Depression, Anxiety and How to Overcome It.*

Anxiety and depression are life long illnesses. They are can be hard to detect, and often go unnoticed for years. Once they have developed, they are can be very hard to treat. Making the issue more complicated, treatment is going to be slightly different for each and every individual. You now have a knowledgebase of information about anxiety and depression. You have generalized theories for why depression and anxiety are so common in modern society, and you have a toolbox to refer to treat these illnesses.

There is no shame to having anxiety or depression. They are conditions that are not the fault of our actions; there is nothing that we could have done to prevent these illnesses. I have that you take the suggestions in this book to heart. All of the tips that I have provided have greatly helped me. Today, I feel better at work and am more relaxed in social situations. The advice in this book may work, but remember that is not an instantaneous result. You will need to work hard to remove anxiety and depression from your life, and realistically the best we can ever hope for is to minimize complications caused by anxiety and depression.

Use the advice in chapters four and five. Most of what I have provided are actions that you can take yourself. Remember that anxiety and depression might not be something you can tackle by yourself. If you feel that you need the help of others, seek aid in the form of a therapist or psychiatrist. I highly recommend speaking to a therapist before moving to a psychiatrist. A therapist will seek to solve your problems through communication, whereas a psychiatrist will more than likely want to offer medication. In the end, if medication is what it takes, do not feel afraid to take medicine to treat these conditions; millions of Americans have found success through medication, myself included.

Thank you and good luck!

Cognitive Behavioral Therapy Mastery

How to Master Your Brain and Your Emotions to Overcome Depression, Anxiety and Phobias

© Copyright 2017 by Ryan James - All rights reserved.

The following Book is reproduced below with the goal of providing information that is as accurate and reliable as possible. Regardless, purchasing this Book can be seen as consent to the fact that both the publisher and the author of this book are in no way experts on the topics discussed within and that any recommendations or suggestions that are made herein are for entertainment purposes only. Professionals should be consulted as needed prior to undertaking any of the action endorsed herein.

This declaration is deemed fair and valid by both the American Bar Association and the Committee of Publishers Association and is legally binding throughout the United States.

Furthermore, the transmission, duplication or reproduction of any of the following work including specific information will be considered an illegal act irrespective of if it is done electronically or in print. This extends to creating a secondary or tertiary copy of the work or a recorded copy and is only allowed with express written consent of the Publisher. All additional right reserved.

The information in the following pages is broadly considered to be a truthful and accurate account of facts, and as such any inattention, use or misuse of the information in question by the reader will render any resulting actions solely under their purview. There are no scenarios in which the publisher or the original author of this work can be in any fashion deemed liable for any hardship or damages that may befall them after undertaking information described herein.

Additionally, the information in the following pages is intended only for informational purposes and should thus be thought of as universal. As befitting its nature, it is presented without assurance regarding its prolonged validity or interim quality.

Trademarks that are mentioned are done without written consent and can in no way be considered an endorsement from the trademark holder.

Introduction

Congratulations on downloading this book and thank you for doing so.

The following chapters will discuss simple strategies that you can use to become a true master at cognitive behavioral therapy, one of the most commonly used techniques in the treatment of anxiety, depression, and phobias.

There are plenty of books on this subject on the market, thanks again for choosing this one! Every effort was made to ensure it is full of as much useful information as possible, please enjoy!

Chapter 1: A Brief Look at cognitive behavioral therapy

To be able to truly master cognitive behavioral therapy and all of the techniques that come with it, you need to first understand how the brain works, what anxiety or depression can do to it and how cognitive behavioral therapy is actually able to help your brain. To get the most use out of this book, it is a good idea to read *Cognitive Behavioral Therapy: The Definitive Guide to Understanding Your Brain, Depression, Anxiety and How to Overcome It*. That is the first book in this series and will give you *all* of the basics that you need to know to be able to get started on truly becoming a master of your anxiety and the cognitive behavioral therapy that will help you to become a happier, healthier person.

While you should have learned most of what you need to know about the way that anxiety and depression can affect your brain in the last book, this chapter is going to serve as a refresher course on the way that they work and the way that cognitive behavioral therapy is able to help you with each of them.

Anxiety and depression are both closely related and are often the result of a misfire or an action that was inappropriate for the situation. For example, someone may experience anxiety because they had a surge of adrenaline driving their vehicle to the store two miles down the road. They would then begin to associate driving with adrenaline. The fight or flight response would kick in each time that they got behind the wheel of a car and they would feel that their life was being threatened. It could then escalate to an extreme point, and that is the way that anxiety works. It tricks the brain into thinking that normal situations are dangerous. This fight or flight response is a leftover mechanism from the days when humans *did* need to either run (from a predator) or prepare to fight (that same predator). While most people do not need to run up a tree to get away from a bear or prepare to kill it with their spears, the surge of adrenaline will still come from normal situations, and it is something that people need to overcome.

The same principles work with depression without the Paleolithic feel attached to it. Humans are designed to feel emotions. Sadness is one of the most extreme emotions that a person can feel and the brain will sometimes get caught in a loop and tell someone to continuously feel sad. This can be triggered by anything – from a change in physical status to a new job to even…anxiety! The brain will tell the person that he or she needs to become sad for reasons that would normally be considered "every day" and the person would get stuck there. That is the way that depression works in the brain.

cognitive behavioral therapy works to combat both of these in the way that it deals with the brain. The point of cognitive behavioral therapy is to trick the brain into getting into a new pattern and retrain it how to think like a "normal" brain. Cognitive behavioral therapy is as simple as a training method that will teach a person by retraining their brain to think in a way that makes sense. When a person goes through cognitive behavioral therapy, it can sometimes be uncomfortable physically, but more commonly it is uncomfortable emotionally.

The good news is that cognitive behavioral therapy is *very* effective at treating anxiety, depression, and phobias. It has been proven to be one of the best ways to combat the problems that come with each of these disorders, and it is actually one of the fastest ways to normalize the brain. cognitive behavioral therapy is not one standalone method but a combination of many different things that will allow you to overcome the problems that your brain has. Each of these methods has been proven to work and have slightly different approaches but will be able to accomplish the same thing – overcoming anxiety, depression or phobias.

A word of caution: not all mental disorders are able to be treated with cognitive behavioral therapy, and you should first get the clearance of a medical professional before you try to start any type of behavioral therapy on your own. Be sure that you have anxiety, depression or phobias before you start cognitive behavioral therapy because these problems can mimic other mental disorders. It is always best to follow the advice of your physician and continue taking any medication that has been prescribed to you if you have a mental disorder. Starting a program, stopping medication or trying to "fix" yourself without the approval of a doctor can be detrimental to your health.

Chapter 2: Multimodal Therapy

One of the most comprehensive ways that people can use cognitive behavioral therapy is through Multimodal therapy. This is a type of therapy that utilizes several different avenues to allow people to see the different ways that they are affected by their anxiety and depression. Once they figure out how their anxiety or depression shapes each of these areas of their lives, they can begin working on the healing process and making sure that they are able to overcome the problems that they have. Multimodal is the way that a person's behavior, affects, sensations, images, cognition, interpersonal relationships, and dependence are all affected by anxiety or depression.

Behavior

The behavior that is seen in people who have anxiety and/or depression is different depending on what they are dealing with and to what degree. It is important to note that there are many different behavior problems that can come from both anxiety and depression. These include:

- Childish acts
- Inappropriate acts
- Extreme obedience
- Destructive behavior
- Compulsive behavior
- High levels of self-control

While all of these behaviors are not uncommon to see in people who are not dealing with anxiety and depression, they can be exacerbated by the disorders. The main characteristic of this is that the behaviors are negative and can cause serious problems for the person who is doing the behaviors.

The multimodal way of treating these behaviors is to figure out what they are and directly address them to figure out what type of problems they could be causing as a secondary result of the disorders that are affecting the brain.

Affects

There is always a way that anxiety and depression can affect a person but when dealing with a multimodal type of treatment, the effect is the intensity of which emotions are felt, and actions are done. A person who has anxiety may have a much more intense effect than someone who has depression, and it can be a problem in both instances.

In general, someone who does not have a mental disorder would not generally feel very strong emotions. The emotions that people who have anxiety and depression feel are actually what can cause them to seek out therapy in the first place – they may be concerned that their emotions are out of control.

It is important to note that just recognizing these emotions and even, in some instances, talking about them, will not be able to change the way that they are in the brain. It is something that takes several levels of therapy to get to and can sometimes take a longer time to be able to address it. There are different emotions that are associated with the intensity, and that can change the way that the person who has anxiety or depression does things.

Sensations

These are the physical symptoms that are felt during a bout of anxiety or depression. The most common are:

- Sweating
- Tension
- Physical pain

- Nausea
- Increased heart rate
- Shaking
- Fidgeting

These are common during an anxiety attack or even during a dark time while someone is depressed. They can affect the way that a person does things and it can be harder for a person to concentrate when these physical symptoms are going on.

The multimodal aspect of this is that one of the other things that are happening – like images or cognition – can cause each of these physical symptoms to manifest. Sometimes, though, there are problems and a person may feel these for no reason at all. They may not know it, but there could have been something that did actually trigger them to feel these feelings.

It is important to note that the sensations are not going to be fixed by fighting them. The person who feels the sensations should accept them for what they are because trying to fight them can actually make them worse. By acceptance, a person will be able to start the healing process that goes along with the therapy.

Images

People who have anxiety and depression are often able to see the worst possible scenario of a situation. This is imagery by which they associate nearly everything with, and it can be a problem or a benefit. If someone is constantly thinking about the worst case scenario, they may avoid doing simple things like driving or going to the store. This leads to even higher anxiety and depression levels for that person.

The way in which images can be the *good* thing is that once someone learns to channel the imagery in their mind and turn it into a positive thing, it can help them to solve problems. It is not uncommon for creative people to be depressed or have anxiety because of the bold images that they often see.

Cognition

Self-talk and the inner voice are the easiest ways to understand cognition in any person. A person with anxiety or depression will often use negative self-talk, and they will have an inner voice that is not very strong. They may struggle with the thoughts that they do have or even their opinions of themselves.

When using multimodal therapy, the point is to try to replace the negative cognition with positive. This is done through various methods including using images to make things more positive for the person who is experiencing negative self-talk.

Interpersonal

There are many relationships issues that people may experience when they have anxiety or depression. It is something that can have a negative effect on the way that things are done and the way that they interact. With multimodal therapy, a person can change their interpersonal relationships by learning how to cope with things in a healthy way instead of being codependent to another person.

Dependence

When it comes to people who have anxiety or depression, there is a higher chance that they will have dependencies on chemicals or emotions. It can affect the way a person chooses to do things, but it can be different depending on the way that a person functions. Whether they are able to sleep, use drugs or even depend on another person will all be related to the anxiety and depression. Multimodal therapy can change this by creating different cognitive patterns and negative associations with the dependency items. It is something that will change the way that the person is able to function and make them better able to deal with things without reaching for something that they had previously been dependent on.

The main idea of multimodal therapy is to combine each of the different aspects of negative thinking and negative behaviors and replace them with positive things. It is important that the person doing this do it in *all* areas and pay close attention to the way that each of the different aspects is connected to each other.

Chapter 3: Looking at Reality

Trying to adjust to a reality that isn't ideal can be difficult for some people, but it is something that needs to be done to be able to overcome anxiety and depression. People who are able to overcome it are those who want to make sure that they are doing the right thing and that they are not the victim of their past. By looking at the past and overcoming it, reality therapy is able to change the way that the present is handled. People who choose to overcome it will no longer be victims of their past but will, instead, be able to flourish in their new role as someone who has defeated an anxiety or depression disorder.

Right and Wrong

The first thing that reality therapy will focus on is whether or not something is right or wrong. The therapy aims to take a look at the way that things can change and the different aspects of it. The person should decide whether something is right or wrong.

When using reality therapy, the person needs to listen to their own inner voice. Most are surprised to find that it is difficult to think of what *they* believe instead of what they have been told to believe or what they have been told is right or wrong. This is something that will change the way that they do things, though, and it will give them a better chance at doing more for themselves. When they are able to use their own inner voice instead of the voice of someone else who has told them how to think, they will be able to make a decision on what is right and what is wrong.

The easiest way to do this is to create a list of things that are in the moral gray area. The list can be anything that is close to them or related to them, but it should be something that has strong moral implications. When the person looks at it, they should decide the black and white area that the previously gray area item went into. It is something that will change depending on the situation, and it will give them a new perspective on the way that they should feel about things instead of just going off of whatever they have been told to feel.

Responsibility

When a person experiences anxiety or depression, they may feel like they can place the blame on something or someone else. The biggest thing that they need to be able to do is learn how to take responsibility for their own mental illness. It can be difficult, but it is something that can be done with a little bit of practice.

To be able to take responsibility of their mental disorder, they need to look at the *whys* of having it. Do they think that they have it from their parents? Because they had a traumatic youth? Because they don't know how to function in social situations? By looking at each of these reasons, it is clear to see that they are putting the blame on something other than themselves.

It can be really difficult to get to this point, but it is a good thing once it happens. If a person is able to look at themselves and say: "I have depression as a result of my own brain reacting differently" they will then be able to take care of the problem and make sure that they are fixing their depression.

The difference in responsibility and blame is that a person who is responsible for something aims to fix the problem that is currently happening. A person who is blaming someone for their problems will not want to fix the current problem but will, instead, be focused on the problems of their past. They will want to blame these people for the problems that they have.

Realism

Understanding the way that the world works is one of the most important qualities that come along with trying to make reality therapy work. The person who has anxiety or depression may be stuck in the past in their own head, and that is something that can be a problem. By taking a step back and looking at the different things that can be done in the present, they are going to give themselves a better chance at reality. It is a great way for people to make sure that they are getting the most out of reality and that they are able to provide themselves with the best opportunity possible.

The easiest way to do this is to keep track of each of the things that are actually going on. A person should write down the different positive things that are happening in their daily lives. By keeping track of this, they can, essentially, pull themselves out from the muck that is in the past and can be holding them down. It is a good idea to make sure that the things they are focusing on, in reality, are positive.

By making sure that they know what is going on with reality and that things are happening all around them, they will have a better chance at moving on from the past, doing the right thing and joining everyone in reality.

Overcoming It

Each of these methods can make reality therapy truly work for anyone who is suffering from anxiety or depression. It is one of the easiest therapy options regarding logistics, but it can be hard for people to make sure that they are truly pulling themselves out of the past. Because of the problems that come with the different therapy methods, people may want to choose reality as a way to make sure that they are doing things the right way.

While it may be uncomfortable to focus on the present instead of the past, it is one of the first steps of healing. With reality therapy, people can make sure that they are getting the most out of each situation and that they are doing the best job possible at becoming a better, happier person.

Reality therapy does not always work the way that you want it to. It may take some extra time and may be a problem for people who are in different situations. It can be extremely detrimental for people to think that they are going to be able to do different things in a world that is truly real, instead of thinking about the different ways that they will not be able to do things. Because of this, a person should always be cautious when they are using reality therapy. It can be painful to look at the past and overcome it, but it can also be beneficial for people who want to be able to do more with the past and with the different things that they have going on at the present time.

Chapter 4: Acceptance and Commitment

Unlike many of the other cognitive behavioral therapy techniques that you will learn throughout the course, acceptance and commitment therapy does not get rid of the negative thoughts that you have. Instead, it focuses on accepting the thoughts and learning to manage them through commitment. There are two different approaches that people can take when they are using the acceptance and commitment technique to overcome anxiety and depression. The two techniques that are used are FEAR and ACT which are acronyms that stand for different steps that you can take.

Fuse Your Thoughts

This is where you are going to stop your thoughts from "running." If you have thoughts that will not stop and are just going around in circles, you need to fuse them together to make sure that you are able to stop them. By fusing your thoughts, you are going to slow down the thinking process which can put a halt on the fight or flight response. It is a way to make sure that you are getting the most out of the situation and it will allow you the chance to make sure that you can take a step back to do the next part of the process.

Expand on What Has Happened

Take an outside look at everything that is going on. Did you get in the car to drive and started having physical symptoms? Did you try to do something normal and it turned into a big production? Were you uncomfortable in a social situation? By taking a look at what has happened, you will allow yourself the chance to expand on the experience and what is going on. You will make yourself objective to the situation instead of passive where the situation is affecting you. Expand on what you know about the experience and what you are doing with the experience. Try to figure out the rational explanation for the experience and the way that it is going to happen to you.

When you are struggling with anxiety or depression, this can be one of the hardest things that you will need to do. It will also be the most helpful to you during this time, and you can make sure that you are getting the most out of the experience by expanding on it.

Avoid Your Senses

When you are struggling with depression or an anxiety attack, your senses are going to be reacting to the fight or flight system in your body. They are going to be doing different things that you may not understand. During these times, it is best to avoid your senses. Do not pay attention to the fact that your fingers feel like they are tingling, that you have bad taste in your mouth or that your sixth sense just feels off. It is your brain trying to trick you.

Instead of focusing on your senses, you can avoid your senses by trying to focus on different actions. Pay attention to the actions that you are doing and what is going on around you. Do not run away from your senses but, instead, put them on the back burner and try to make sure that they are not interrupting what you need to get done.

Reframe Your Situation

This in no way means that you need to run from the situation or change it to do something else. You need to only look at it in a different light. Spin it so that it is positive. If you have to give a big presentation at work and your anxiety is getting the best of you, think of it in a positive way. At least you have work to give a presentation at, and nearly everyone has done it before so it can't be that bad.

The reframing process can be hard, but it will give you a chance to make sure that you are getting the most out of the situation. It will also teach you how to look at things more objectively instead of just running from things that might be going on while you are having anxiety or you are depressed.

Accept and Focus

The first part of the ACT plan is to accept the emotions that you are having no matter how negative they are. Think about them as thoughts that are coming to your head and let them flow through it. Allow them the space to give you some worry. By accepting that something bad *could* happen, you will give yourself the chance to make things actually happen in your life. It will also give you the chance to do more with what you are planning. Accepting negative thoughts causes them to lose their power within your own mind.

Once you have accepted the thoughts, focus on them and what the worst case scenario would be. What would be so bad if you did mess up the presentation? What would be the problem if you *did* have an anxiety attack while driving? Each of these things is truly not that bad and can make a difference in your life depending on the different things that you have going through your mind.

Create Your Plan

Decide what you are going to do with the thoughts that you just accepted. Are you going to take them and act on them by not driving or not doing the presentation? Are you going to make it harder to think about the different situations that you could be in? Are you going to ask the thoughts to leave?

Having a plan in place for negative thoughts is the only way that you will be able to overcome them. Make sure that you know what you want to do with them and where you want them to go. Give yourself time to plan your negative thoughts *before* they happen so that you will be prepared. Handle the thoughts according to what you want your actions to be and what you want to be able to overcome. This will give you a chance at making sure that you can get over the negative thoughts and that you can make your life a better one.

Time to Act

Once you have accepted the negative thoughts as normal and something that will just always be there and you have made the plan that you wanted to be able to put into place, you can then act on that plan. Make sure that you know what is going on and what you are going to be able to do with your negative thoughts. Each of these thoughts will make things harder for you but having the plan in place will give you an opportunity to act.

If you deliberately do this for each of the negative thoughts that you have, you will eventually learn how to do it automatically. This is a coping method and something that can be used very easily once you have an idea of how to do it. You will be able to retrain your brain so that it automatically accepts all of your negative thoughts, uses the plans that you have put into place and acts on the plans that are there. It will allow you to overcome the negative thoughts just by accepting them.

Chapter 5: Functional Analytics

The functional analytic form of cognitive behavioral therapy focuses on noticing the way that someone does something, looking at the way that the person responds and changing the way that they respond to it. This is something that can change depending on the situation and will make things better for the person who is undergoing the therapy. This method is difficult to use on your own, but it can be done with someone else who can look at the way that you do things.

Negative

When a person has a negative response to something, that is what needs to be noticed, accepted and changed. This can be a negative result to anything from having to get up to work to driving their car to talk in front of people. The person who is helping out with this type of therapy needs to figure out what brings negative emotions to the person who is undergoing the therapy. This will allow him or her to make sure that things are done in a controlled environment.

The helper should then give the person an idea of something that will bring about the negative behaviors. This can be something as simple as saying, "I can't help you anymore" to "You have to drive 1,200 miles, you have no choice." The negative response will then kick in, and the person who is receiving the therapy may light up in different areas physically. They will also have an emotional response but it is a good idea to focus only on the physical since that is something that will be much easier for them to change the way that they do things when something negative happens to them or in any other situation that they may be in that could cause them to feel anxiety or become depressed.

Positive

The opposite works for things that are positive for the person. The helper should tell the person who is receiving therapy something that is positive like "I bought you some flowers for no reason" or "You have an extra 100 dollars in your checking account." This will also cause the person to light up physically. They will be able to then notice the changes that their body goes through when they are doing different things, and it will give them the chance to see that they do have the capability to have a positive attitude.

The helper needs to encourage this behavior for the person to be able to truly see that it is making a difference. When the helper praises the person for having a positive reaction, it will show the person that things can get better and that they are able to enjoy things. This is an especially helpful technique for people who are depressed or who are going through a particularly bad bout of anxiety.

When the helper shows them that they are capable of positive behavior and encouraging it, they will show them that things can get better and that they will be able to apply this to different situations. The more positive a person is, the better able they are to track their physical reaction to positive things.

Bringing Change

The biggest change that should occur is that the person works on the physical symptoms when there is something that is negative going on with the different things that they have. When a person clenches their teeth or scrunches up their eyebrows in response to being told that they are going to have to do one more work assignment, they will be able to see that they are reacting physically. It is something that needs to change, though, and once they are able to see what they are doing and how they are reacting to the different negative situations, they can start to change.

The change needs to happen by first getting back to a neutral place. When the person notices that they are reacting, they can take a pause and bring themselves back down to the way that things are going. It is something that will make them better able to react to these situations and will allow them the chance to make sure that they are not reacting in a physical sense.

By noticing and overcoming each of these things, a person will be able to make sure that they are able to overcome the emotional problems. The first thing that usually happens is physical, and the subsequent actions are usually emotional. Once you overcome the physical part of reacting to a situation, you will then be able to overcome the emotional part of the different things that are going on.

Praise

The praise part is just as important in the negative areas as it is in the positive areas. The person who is helping out should always make sure that he or she is encouraging the person who is able to drop back down to neutral when they experience the negative emotion. This is something that will need to make things better and will allow them to see that they are doing things the right way. It is a way to show them that their behavior can be changed and that they are capable of making their own lives better without the help of nonsense.

When the helper notices that the physical reaction is gone, he or she should try their hardest to show the person who is undergoing the therapy that they are going to be able to continue doing that. By telling them "good job" or showing them that things will get better, they will be able to make sure that they are doing things the right way and that they are getting the most out of the experience.

It is a good idea to notice the way that a person is encouraged once they are praised. If they receive enough praise when they do something positive and again when they are able to drop back down to neutral, they will associate the neutral position with something that is positive. It will be a good way for them to change the way that they do things without ever even having to try.

Keeping it Up

Once a person has learned what they are able to do with their positive attitude and the praise that comes along with doing things the right way, they will be able to continue that behavior. While it may seem like they are only teaching themselves how to do something the right way, they are actually showing their brain how it should be reacting to different situations.

The brain is a powerful thing that people with anxiety and depression need to overcome. While it can be helpful, it can also be detrimental. If you constantly bring praise and teach yourself the right way to react to different stimuli, even normal things, you can show your brain what it is supposed to be doing. The trick is to make it think that it is doing the right thing and that will, in turn, make the manifestation that comes about in your own physical symptoms the correct way that they are supposed to be.

Chapter 6: Cognitive Processing

The way to which the mind responds to an event or other stimuli is powerful and can cause a person to become "set in their ways" with their ability to do different things. Because of this, cognitive processing therapy is sometimes used to change the way that a person thinks of a certain situation, feeling or even a past event. It is an effective cognitive therapy technique, and it allows the person to overcome the problems that they had in the past. The first part of healing an anxiety or depressive disorder is to move forward from things that have happened in the past and that have been detrimental to the person.

Learning About It

To be able to successfully learn the right way to overcome the problems that a person has with anxiety or depression, they must first look at the past. They need to see what type of problems they had in the past, the way that their problems affected them and how they shaped them for the future of everything that they are going to be able to do. Since a person needs to get over their past before they can move toward their future, cognitive processing focuses on learning about the past and how it shaped that person.

When someone is dealing with their past, it can be quite painful. Therapists who use this method like to take the process slow and find out as much as they can about the past of the person to get the person talking about it and find out what triggers them in the process. This part of learning about the traumatic events or other past issues usually takes around four weeks for a therapist to get through. This is the first stage of the process, and each of the three stages is divided evenly.

However long it will take the therapist, and the person who is receiving therapy to get through each of the problems is dependent on this first one and the length of time that it takes.

A therapist will likely ask their patient to come up with ideas about the past. Some people who are going through therapy might find that they actually have repressed memories of the past especially if it was traumatic. This is something that can be detrimental as well as good. While they are trying to get through these repressed memories, they may find something that is the true trigger to their depression and anxiety. It will allow them to see what it is and that they have one which is the first part of getting better and moving forward with their life.

If someone is able to figure out all of their repressed memories and all of the information that they hold, they will be able to learn as much as possible with their emotions and the problems that they have. It will allow them the chance to move on and make their lives better.

Accepting and Processing

Once a person has learned as much as possible about the events in their past and what has created this sort of anxiety or depression state, they will be able to begin the acceptance process. While finding the memories and looking at them clearly was certainly hard during the first step, this can be even harder because they need to "come to terms" with the problems that they had and make sure that they are doing things the right way for their memories.

Once they have taken the time to confront them, they will then need to make sure that they are accepting them. Are they still trying to repress these memories? Or, are they looking them in the face and acknowledging that they are there and they are making problems for the people who need to "get over" the hump of traumatic memories? Once they have learned how to, essentially, look their bad memories in the eye, they will then be able to say that they have officially accepted the memories.

One of the biggest parts of this process is not putting the blame on another person or situation that the person is in while they are repressing memories and trying to recall them. For example, someone may be tempted to think about a traumatic event and blame it on their parents, the person who was with them or even themselves. They need to let go of this blame. They will never have full acceptance of the memory and the trauma that it caused until they are ready to stop blaming someone else, something else or even themselves for the problem. Placing blame with a cognitive processing will not fix the problem or even put a name to the problem, it will just push it further into the context of memories.

As with the first step, it can be expected that this step will take about four weeks. With cognitive processing, therapists do not like to move fast. This is because they need to make sure that each step of the process is being done the correct way and that the patient has moved from one step to the next in the proper way before they can begin it. They will not be able to be successful with any of the steps if they are not able to get through the first or second step.

Getting Through It

Once someone has found the memories and accepted them, they may think that they are out of the woods and that they are healed of their anxiety and depression. This is not the case, though, and it is the point at which many people trip up and lose their own ability to be able to deal with the memories and the things that they have because of them. They need to continue to learn how to *not* repress memories and to keep things light for themselves. It is important to make sure that they know how to get through the situations that they are in and that they are making sure that they will not do it again.

After the cognitive processing is done, the person's brain will be trained to not repress memories and to keep themselves as levelheaded as possible in all situations. The memories that they had, even the ones they did not know about, will no longer be triggers and they will not have to worry about the different problems that come with the triggers. Cognitive processing is effective in that it promotes someone's good memories and allows them to accept the bad while not bringing them up all of the time.

It is important to note that there are many problems that can come with memory repression. This is especially true if someone has anxiety and/or depression due to sexual assault, PTSD or something similar. The memories can be painful and bring them up out of a repressed state can make things even worse for the person. That is why it is important to consult with a mental health professional before trying to do cognitive processing therapy. It can sometimes be detrimental and having the help of a professional will allow the therapy to be more successful.

Chapter 7: Reprocessing and EMDT

Some cognitive behavioral therapy methods work with the mental aspect of the brain while others work with the physical. It can sometimes be hard to cope, especially when anxiety is spiraling out of control. People need to learn how to process that and figure out a coping method that works right for them. The reprocessing therapy works by focusing on the movement of the eyes and how it is able to help a person reprocess all of the information that they have stored in their own brain depending on the different ways that things will be able to go for them and the way that things can be improved when it comes to their abilities.

History

When you are planning on using reprocessing, there are several things that you will first need to take a look at. As with all things that you do in cognitive behavioral therapy, you will need to look into the past to find the memories that can function as triggers for your anxiety and depression. You need to keep track of these memories because this is how you are going to make a change to the triggers that you have the memories that you have made in the past.

Relaxing

You can start to relax the first time that you try to do reprocessing. You will need to take time when you are not stressed about anything and notice the sensations that you feel. Relax your eye muscles, the rest of your head muscles and everything else so that you can make sure that you are getting the most out of the situation. It will allow you the chance to ensure that you are relaxed. Keep track of these feelings. You can then use this when you are having a stressful time.

Cognition Scale

The cognition scale is used to see how well you can relax while you are thinking about memory as a trigger or while there is a trigger that is present and making you tense. It is expected that you would be a 1 or a 2 on the scale when you are first getting started with reprocessing, but by the end of treatment, you should be at the highest point on the scale, a 7. This takes some time and a lot of positive imagery to be able to conquer in the way that you need to start healing.

Retraining

There are several steps to the process, but the retraining part is what you will be able to focus on the most. This is what will make things work the right way for you and will allow you the chance to make sure that you have mastered reprocessing. Once you have learned how to do this, your brain will be trained to immediately start associating the relaxation techniques with the trigger that previously made you feel anxious or upset in any way.

Strengthening

While it may seem that having your brain automatically associate good things with the stimuli you previously experienced in a negative light, this is not always the best way to be able to handle the situation. You will need to learn how to do this in a way that makes more sense and so that you can continue to strengthen the belief that you have that this is, in fact, a positive thing. Doing this will allow you to continue using this technique and will allow you to keep the anxiety at bay for years even after you have finished it.

The easiest way for you to continue strengthening your beliefs is to consistently go back to that place of relaxation. While your brain is still able to do this on its own, you will want to make sure that you do it on a cognitive level as well. You do not need to do this every time that you think that something is going wrong, but when you begin to get stressed or notice stimuli affecting you, you should try to go back to the place of relaxation. There is nothing new to learn when it comes to strengthening, but you will need to remember to practice what you have already learned.

Lingering Sensations

If there are any types of sensations that could cause a person to feel like they are going to become anxious again or that they are going to start to stress, there needs to be a plan in place to be able to handle them. This could be anything from mild stress to tension to need to be surrounded by people or anything else that could signal oncoming anxiety. When a person starts to feel this, they need to take their time and specifically relax for the benefit of themselves. This is the only way that they can get through it.

One thing that many therapists will suggest that their clients do is to go looking for these thoughts and these feelings. When they start to feel a twinge of something bad happening, they need to latch onto that and make sure that they are trying to figure out how to react to it so that they will be able to do more. They can benefit from this because they will be able to learn as much as possible about what makes it happen and what they can do to make it relax. Even years after therapy has been completed, you can benefit from seeking out lingering sensations and quashing them.

Logging It

Throughout all of the different things that go on with reprocessing, you need to log them. You should figure out what you are doing, what you feel and the sensations that you have so that you will be able to learn as much as possible about the different things that are going on. It is important to log it and keep track of it so that you can learn what your triggers are, how to relax through them and how to make sure that you are doing things the right way when you are trying to fix your anxiety and your depression.

Determination

Since you have logged all of the information, it will be easy for both you and your therapist to go back and see what made the determination on whether or not you were going to get anxious over something. You may find that simply logging the information can help with anxiety, but you will need to determine *why* you are anxious, what you have done to fix it and what has worked for you to be able to get through any type of situation or trigger.

The biggest aspect of reprocessing is the physical aspect. Averting your eyes to something else, allowing them to look inward at what you are doing and giving yourself a chance to notice the physical symptoms of what is happening when a trigger is brought to your attention are all ways that you can redirect your own attention away from the different aspects of your life. It is something that you will need to be able to do and use to your advantage when it comes time to continue with the reprocessing and with your own life while trying to overcome the anxiety and depression.

Chapter 8: Rational Therapy Method

The rational look at cognitive behavioral therapy is to make sure that things are being done in a rational way and that the reactions to each of the triggers are handled on a trigger by trigger basis. Rational therapy is a way to make sure that a person reacts in a way that is appropriate instead of an overreaction or a misfire in the reaction to a stimulus that is given.

The Trigger

With rational therapy, the therapist will start by having a subject look at one trigger at a time. Once they are able to overcome one of the triggers, it will then be easier for them to fix the other triggers and they will be able to make sure that they are getting the most out of the situation that they are in without having to worry about the way that the trigger is going to affect them. They will first need to bring up one of their triggers and figure out what happens to them when the trigger is brought about.

Bringing up triggers can be difficult to do when you are not in the situation so if you want to do this, you should be prepared to make a log when you are feeling particularly depressed or anxious. Write down what made you feel that way and what you think did it. If you cannot think of a specific thing on the outside of your head, you can look at the inside of it and see if it was something like an obsessive thought or an intrusive attitude that made you think of the things that you were going to do. It can be anything on the inside *or* the outside of your head that can trigger your feelings.

Stimulating It

Once you have felt that trigger, coax it as much as possible. If you are *trying* to make something trigger you, it can be even harder because the chances of that happening are very slim. The brain will only do it when you are not paying attention and when you are unable to see it coming. Since the triggers can cause organic responses, try to get the triggers to do as much as possible when it comes time to you making sure that things are going the right way and when you are doing different things with your own triggers.

It is a good idea to try to make sure that you can see, physically, what is going on with your response to the trigger. Do you shake? Does your heart rate increase? Do you sweat? Each of these things is responses to triggers and are generally an overreaction of the brain to something that is completely harmless because the brain wants you to think that there is something to be scared of or something that you will not be able to get to when it comes to a certain point. This is known as fight or flight, and it is what you are trying to overcome.

Replacing It

After you have figured out what the trigger is and how it can have a negative effect on you with the different symptoms, try to replace them. Instead of paying attention to your sweaty hands when you see a dog coming toward you on the street, look at a picture of something funny or repeat a mantra to yourself. You can do many different things to replace the negative responses to stimuli but always make sure that they are positive and they are going to be able to help you get the negative response.

It is a good idea to make sure that you are doing the most for yourself by always replacing them with something positive. From the time that you decide that you are going to be rational about your emotions, you can start to replace things that are negative with things that are positive. Instead of telling yourself that you are going to die, tell yourself that you are sitting on a beach and listening to the waves crash. This is the "happy place" technique that many people use when they have to do something uncomfortable, like getting a shot or having to do a scary interview. By figuring out how to get to that "happy place," you will always be able to replace negative emotions.

Perfectionism

Most people who suffer from anxiety and depression do so because they are not able to live up to the standards that they have set for themselves and they do not know how to handle it. They overreact when they are not perfect or when something does not go the exact way that they want it to go. It is something that will not be able to help them and something that will not make a difference in the way that things are done.

When you are able to overcome perfectionism, you will be able to overcome the negative reactive behavior that you have to different stimuli. If you know how to accept things when they are not exactly perfect, you will be able to accept the fact that people do not always do the exact things that they want to be able to do. You may not be able to get the perfect reaction that you want, but you will be able to react in a more rational sense.

Getting rid of perfectionism can be hard especially if that is something that you have always done, but once you conquer this aspect of your life, you will be on your way to getting over the problems that you have with your irrational reactions. It can be difficult to find a balance between not being a perfectionist and being lazy so make sure that you are careful to not go to the other end of the spectrum.

Putting it Into Practice

All of these things will be able to add up and make rational sense to you once you begin to do them. Learn the right way to become more rational before you make the decision to do anything else and that will give you a chance to do better at the way that things are going for your anxiety and depression. It can sometimes be hard to be able to do the same type of things with the way that you are reacting but know that doing that will help you to overcome both anxiety and depression.

Learning how to be more rational and to make emotionally rational decisions will allow you to live a more normal life. Once you take the time to make sure that you are as rational as possible, it will give you a chance to do that when it comes to triggers and other things that are going on in your life. You will find that you will be able to react more normally to triggers than before. You will not need to worry about having to fight or run away from a situation just because that is what your brain is telling you to do. Fixing your brain with anxiety is as easy as learning how to be more rational.

Chapter 9: Dialectical Therapy

As you may have imagined due to the name, dialectical therapy is a type of talk therapy that will allow you the chance to make sure that you are moving forward from the phobias and depressive states that you may get into. This type of therapy is particularly helpful for people who obsess over problems that they may have and for people who want to be able to make sure that they are able to make the right decision. Changing behavior with dialectical therapy is done almost exclusively from within, and it is what some people refer to as mindfulness while using techniques that will teach you more about your inner self.

Looking Around

By taking a minute to look around at your surroundings, you can bring yourself out of your head. While it is important to help yourself with this method inside of your head, you want to be able to do something that will get you out of the behavior that the brain has set up in response to the different stimuli that are all around you. It is important to make sure that the brain is able to do as much as possible with what you are doing and looking at the world around you will give the brain a chance to reset or activate itself to form a normal response.

While you are looking around, you should be talking to yourself (in your head, of course) about what you see.

"I see a steering wheel in front of me."

"There is a dog on a leash."

"My child needs my attention."

Each of these things is looking around you and seeing the way that they are in the world. It will also give you a chance to feel like you are in the world outside of your head.

Reporting

Always report to yourself on what you see. Whether you want to do it all in your head or if you find that keeping a journal is easier when you are first getting started will allow you to remember what you see and what you are going to be able to do in the world around you. It can be difficult to get an idea of what is going on so make sure that you are always working hard to figure that out. The specifics of looking around you can be hard to grasp if you are not making the right type of mental note. Always do your best to figure out what is going on and report it directly to yourself.

Since we are using language and our voice for each of these things, it may be a good idea to consider the voice that you are using. Is it one that is calm and reassured? Or, is it one that is shaky and is making you shaky as well? You can change your voice in your head.

Activating the Response

You can activate the response that you have in your head by taking the time to make sure that you are talking to yourself in the best way possible. Figure out what response you *want* to have to the situation and use that to make yourself get through the situation. It may be hard to do this at the moment so you can always try to replicate the situation in your head. Figure out what you are going to say and what you are going to do if something happens and tell yourself that is what you are going to do.

While the point of any cognitive behavioral therapy is to move on from the past, you may find yourself reverting to the past when you are trying to do this. This can be a problem so make sure that you only use current situations or things that can make it harder for you to think about the past.

Avoiding Binary

As you are looking at the word around you and trying to see different things, it may be easy for you to use judgmental terms about the things that you are seeing. You may look at a child who dropped their ice cream cone and say to yourself that is unfair. You should try to avoid this, though. Make sure that you are looking at all of it subjectively. Instead of thinking that it is unfair, think that the child dropped their ice cream cone and that is it.

It can be hard to do this and do not get discouraged if you cannot do it at first but looking at everything subjectively will give your brain a chance to reset and look at everything for what it truly is instead of for the unfairness of it all. Doing this can allow you the chance to make sure that your brain looks at stimuli in a subjective manner.

Focusing on One

If you happen to notice that you cannot stop the inner dialog from moving to something negative, try your hardest to focus on one thing that is positive. This will be the best way for you to be able to get things done and will allow you the chance to make sure that you are getting the best response possible.

When you think about it, this is what your brain does anyway. If you see a dog coming toward you, the only thing that you can think about is a dog attack and what you will look like after it or how bad it will hurt. Instead of doing this, when you look at a dog, think about something positive. Think about how much the owners probably love the dog and continue focusing on that *one* thing. Doing this will allow your brain to switch off the fight or flight response and will slow it down to think more rationally.

Radical Acceptance

When you find that you have a bad response to stimuli or you are being triggered, you should be able to handle the problem by using different techniques. If you are unable to do this, radical acceptance can help. For example, if you are driving and think that you are going to have a heart attack, give into it. Convince yourself that you have one and that you are going to die and then accept it. This is radical, but it is something that will nearly always work. If you take the fear away from something, it takes power away from it too.

Self-Soothing

When you are unable to calm yourself using *any* of the other techniques, you can try some type of self-soothing. This is a skill that is established when people are babies and when they are left to cry for a certain amount of time. They learn to calm themselves through different things, and it allows their thought process to work out the solution to the problem. Whether your self-soothing technique is rubbing a certain spot on your wrist or tapping your feet or even doing something somewhat unhealthy like licking your lips, you can try different things that allow you to soothe yourself when you are scared or worried about something.

Conclusion

Thank for making it through to the end of this book, I hope it was informative and was able to provide you with all of the tools you need to achieve your goals whatever they may be.

The next step is to figure out which cognitive behavioral therapy technique is going to work the best for you and your mental health and start implementing the strategies and take action.

Here's to your success!

Hygge

An Introduction to the Danish Art of Cozy Living

© Copyright 2017 by Amy White and Ryan James

All rights reserved.

The following Book is reproduced below with the goal of providing information that is as accurate and as reliable as possible. Regardless, purchasing this Book can be seen as consent to the fact that both the publisher and the author of this book are in no way experts on the topics discussed within, and that any recommendations or suggestions made herein are for entertainment purposes only. Professionals should be consulted as needed before undertaking any of the action endorsed herein.

This declaration is deemed fair and valid by both the American Bar Association and the Committee of Publishers Association and is legally binding throughout the United States.

Furthermore, the transmission, duplication or reproduction of any of the following work, including precise information, will be considered an illegal act, irrespective whether it is done electronically or in print. The legality extends to creating a secondary or tertiary copy of the work or a recorded copy and is only allowed with express written consent of the Publisher. All additional rights are reserved.

The information in the following pages is broadly considered to be a truthful and accurate account of facts, and as such any inattention, use or misuse of the information in question by the reader will render any resulting actions solely under their purview. There are no scenarios in which the publisher or the original author of this work can be in any fashion deemed liable for any hardship or damages that may befall them after undertaking information described herein.

Additionally, the information found on the following pages is intended for informational purposes only and should thus be considered, universal. As befitting its nature, the information presented is without assurance regarding its continued validity or interim quality. Trademarks that mentioned are done without written consent and can in no way be considered an endorsement from the trademark holder.

Introduction

Congratulations on purchasing your personal copy of *Hygge: An Introduction to the Danish Art of Cozy Living*. Thank you for doing so.

The following chapters will discuss the Danish lifestyle trend that is known as hygge. Perhaps you've heard of hygge before, and want to learn more about it, or perhaps you know nothing about hygge but are excited to learn about how this easygoing mindset and way of life can influence how you live for the better. Either way, the ideas that will be presented in this book are sure to be useful to you in a way that will lead to less stress and more pleasure on a daily basis. As our lives become busier and busier through new developments in technology, it's nice to know that it's still possible to live in a way that promotes togetherness, coziness, and long-term happiness. These concepts are what hygge is all about, and these are the types of nuanced pleasures that hygge can offer your life.

The last chapter is going to discuss how you can create a hygge-optimized fashion sense for you and your closet. The concepts that are going to be presented in this book can be used during any time of the year, and this is similar to some of the other topics that will be discussed in this book. Hygge can infiltrate many aspects of your life, including the activities that you do, the clothes that you wear, the food that you eat, and the mindset that you have about life in general. As you're going to find, hygge is as much about how you design the interior of your home and how you dress yourself as it is about cultivating positive relationships that will leave you and your loved ones feeling supported and happy on a consistent basis.

There are plenty of books on this subject on the market, thanks again for choosing this one! Every effort was made to ensure it is full of as much useful information as possible. Please enjoy!

Congratulations on getting your personal copy of *Hygge: An Introduction to the Danish Art of Cozy Living.*

Enjoy the rest of this book!

Chapter 1: What is Hygge and How Did It Evolve?

Dieting trends seem to always seem to be changing, and it can sometimes be difficult to keep up with the latest dieting fad. Just a few dieting trends include the Atkins Diet, the South Beach Diet, the Wheat Belly Diet, and Jenny Craig. The list goes on, yet the certainty that these diets do in fact work over the long-term is something that can be debated, given the fact that there are so many different diets out there. On the other hand, dieting for the mind is discussed much less than is physical dieting for the body. Finding a balance between the stress that comes with living in the modern technological age and relaxation is often not discussed. Instead, people will typically either become prescribed to medication that will relax them with side effects, or they will simply push through the stress that they feel until they become stress eaters, have a heart attack, or worse. None of these outcomes seem ideal to me.

Hygge As the Answer to Stress Alleviation

Instead of forcing yourself to adapt to the stressful lifestyle that is being pressed upon you by society, another option that you have is to resist it through alternative living techniques. This is where hygge comes into play. Hygge, in the most basic sense, can be defined as the Danish word for a feeling of contentment and comfort. You will see most translations define hygge as being the Danish word for "cozy", but it's important to note that no literal translation actually exists between the two words. Mostly deriving from the Netherlands, many people claim that hygge is what largely contributes to Denmark competing with places like Iceland and

Switzerland as being home to the happiest people on earth.

One of the biggest reasons why the notion of hygge is important to the people of Denmark is because of their exceptionally long winters. Denmark is known for going through periods of up to seventeen hours of darkness per day during the winter, and this darkness brings with it temperatures that are well below zero degrees. These two weather conditions would cause you to initially think that people who live in this type of environment would become incredibly unhappy or even suicidal. Instead, Denmark's reliance on the hygge allows its population to remain entertained, content and happy during even the darkest months of the season.

Comfort Rather than Deprivation

When thinking about how the civilians of Denmark are forced to live in isolation and darkness for months at a time, it's safe to say that they are in a sense isolated from the traditional luxuries that someone who lives in a more temperate area is. For this reason, Danish people as a whole are much less likely to indulge in the types of deprivation techniques that people from both the United States and the United Kingdom are more prone to using. For example, studies have shown that there are far less fad dieters in Denmark than there are in both America and the UK.

Because of the fact that Denmark does suffer from a colder climate throughout the year, people are more focused on making the best of the situation, rather than depriving themselves of anything more than is necessary. From the tendencies that are evident from the behavior of the average Danish person, it's easy to see that a key element of living hygge involves being kind to oneself all of the time. By replacing deprivation with exhibiting kindness to oneself and to others, hygge allows the Danes to feel a greater sense of contentment with their lives, regardless of the specific circumstances in which they find themselves.

The Hygge Lingo

Now that you have a better understanding of how hygge came to be and what this lifestyle values, we will get into how you can pronounce this word properly. You might be thinking that the word hygge is pronounced "Hig-gee", but that is not the case. Instead, if you're looking to pronounce this word properly, you're going to pronounce it "hue-guh". Don't worry, if this pronunciation does not seem all that natural to you, you likely won't be faulted for pronouncing it as it comes naturally to you. In fact, if someone were to challenge your pronunciation of this word, you could simply remind them that you're most comfortable pronouncing it your own way, and in doing so you are completely upholding hygge principles.

Without getting too technical into the Danish language, another term that is sometimes used alongside of the word hygge is the word "hyggeligt". This is an adjective that Danish people use after they've enjoyed time in someone else's home. Even if you don't think that you're ever going to find yourself in a situation where using the term hyggeligt would be appropriate, it is still interesting to see how the term hygge can be used to describe multiple types of comfort in Denmark. The term hyggeligt makes it apparent that the term hygge can expand to include situations where you're comfy with other people. In this way, hygge as a concept is able to abstractly influence your relationships with others in a positive manner. By recognizing that an important part of hygge involves comradery with the people around you, it's possible to see how hygge has become a phenomenon within the Danish community. It doesn't matter what your social status is in Denmark or how much money you make. Everyone within their society is influenced by the principles of hygge, one way or another.

It's the Little Things

As you're going to find after reading the rest of what this book has to offer, a hygge lifestyle emphasizes small, rather than large, gestures. For example, a small act that would be considered hygge in nature would be to sit on your back porch during a cold winter evening, while sipping hot cocoa from a mug that was handmade by a loved one while wearing wool mittens and an extremely warm jacket. Due to the fact that the Danes are the ones who coined the hygge trend, a lot of the imagery surrounding this style emphasizes being in a colder climate; however, if you're looking to expand the definition of hygge to include your particular locale, there's no reason why the coziness that is inherent to hygge necessarily has to mean that you're bundled up in a cold environment.

Chapter 2: Hygge and Happiness

Now that you know what hygge is and how to pronounce it (sort of), this next chapter is going to discuss how you can begin to cultivate the hygge mindset in a way that will generate long-term happiness. Of course, this book is going to discuss actions that you can take that will lead to the outward appearance that you're adapting to the hygge lifestyle; however, without internal recognition of this new way of life, it will be less likely that you'll ever truly adapt to what hygge is all about. Hygge starts in the heart, and that's what this will chapter will discuss, how you can begin to cultivate hygge principles within yourself prior to developing an outwardly hygge lifestyle.

Rethinking the Notion of Perfection

One of the first steps that you can take towards truly understanding what hygge can offer your life is to resist the urge to think in terms of perfection. In a modern Westernized society, it can sometimes seem as if we are constantly pushing ourselves to constantly be better than we already are. While of course, progress can certainly be a positive, it's also possible to surpass a point of where constant progress is attainable. For example, emphasis on body image in the United States has manifested itself into many people becoming fitness-crazed. Additionally, plastic surgery rates have continued to rise all around the world. While the United States is not the first country in terms of the highest plastic surgery rates, it still does rank rather high, coming in sixth out of all the countries in the world. The country where plastic surgery is the most popular is South Korea, followed by Greece, Italy, and Brazil.

It's important to note that there has been a recent rise in plastic surgery in Denmark, but these rates still pale in comparison to the increase in plastic surgery rates in other parts of the world. This increasingly prevalent tendency for women in particular to think that "perfection" is possible from the perspective of their physique is an indication that many societies are caught up in obtaining some type of perfection for themselves. Through hygge, Denmark is able to somewhat set themselves apart from the global phenomenon of perfection that is occurring. The next question that you may have is how exactly is hygge facilitating this type of mindset?

Hygge as an Entry Point for More Self-Indulgence

Instead of focusing on perfection and how to best obtain it, someone who is mindfully involved in cultivating more hygge into his or her life is going to do so by being more self-indulgent. Instead of looking to abstain from the worldly pleasures of life, someone who is wrapped up in becoming more hygge is going to focus inward and take note of what it is that makes them feel cozy, at home, and safe. What this means is that instead of focusing on what is the "norm" in regards to any specific situation, you are instead focusing on how you could feel the most comfortable when a particular situation arises. Let's take a look at some of the ways that you can begin to concretely develop a more self-indulgent mindset for yourself, so that you stop thinking in terms of what is "right" and start thinking more in terms of what's "right for you".

Practice Gratitude Every Day

One of the closest concepts to hygge is gratitude. When you practice gratitude, you're able to appreciate the everyday things in life, rather than only feeling grateful when you're taking a big trip or coming into a lot of money. Cultivating gratitude involves pausing to recognize the world's countless nuances that are both incredibly beautiful as well as special.

When you learn to bring more gratitude into your life, you're going to be able to not only become happier, but also become less materialistic. When someone is materialistic, it means that this person is likely going to try and find happiness through the items that he or she purchases.

This could be as simple as finding happiness in buying new clothes, but it could also be as expensive as buying a new car. The problem with finding happiness in things rather than through gratitude is that the newness of a material possession is going to erode over time. This means that if your happiness is linked to this material possession, your happiness is likely going to be temporary as well. This is why finding gratitude for what you have is important. As it relates to hygge, finding coziness within the smaller things in life goes completely hand-in-hand with being able to fully appreciate those smaller things. In this way, it should be easy to see that if you're simply going through the motions of becoming more hygge without taking the time to learn how to self-indulge, there's a good chance that you're never going to truly "get" it. Below are a few ways that you can start to practice gratitude, if you think that this is an area of your life that could use some work:

1. **Note 5 Things You're Thankful for Each Day**

A great way to jumpstart finding more gratitude in your life involves noting five things that you're thankful for each day. You can jot these five things down in some sort of gratitude journal, but you don't even have to do that! By simply going over five things in your head for which you're thankful each day, you're going to slowly train your brain to be able to pick out the small things that can be make you happier each day, which will lead to greater happiness over time.

2. **Volunteer**

Another way to appreciate what you have is to volunteer

for organizations that are dedicated to helping people who have less than you do. By showing up for these people and providing them with your time, you'll likely be able to truly feel appreciative of all of the goodness that is in your own life.

3. **Avoid Negative Media**

The rise of the internet has made it possible to access countless media sources in a matter of seconds. Not only that, sensationalizing the news has almost become the norm rather than the exception. Gruesome details regarding terrible acts of violence, theft and other types of misdemeanors are literally at our fingertips. Whether or not you're aware of it, these types of details can weigh on the brain and provide you with a sense of pessimism over time. One way to keep the brain more positive is to simply avoid indulging in negative news stories when it's possible.

Indulge in Greater Self-Care

In addition to finding more gratitude in daily life, another way that the Danes use hygge methodology in a way that leads to more happiness is by focusing on self-care. Self-care involves participating in daily life more mindfully and less habitually. A great way that you can begin to become acquainted with the notion of self-care is to create a self-care kit for yourself. For example, this may mean that instead of coming home from work and plopping yourself down on the couch for hours on end, you instead prepare a self-care kit for yourself in advance. This kit may contain things such as warm socks, chocolates, a good book, and maybe even candles. By refocusing your energy on how you can relax properly instead of how you can zone out by watching mindless television, you'll likely find greater pleasure after you come home from a long day of work or school.

Less is More

Lastly, it's important to note that minimalism also has to do with hygge. While minimalism in itself is a separate philosophy from hygge, the two do interact somewhat. For example, hygge advocates for simplicity in your most intimate spaces, rather than a cluttered or unorganized environment. If you feel like you *need* everything in your environment right now, try to look at the concept of simplicity a different way. First, think about what your goals are in terms of how you want to obtain lasting happiness for yourself. In other words, what do you need in order to be happy? Start with this question, and try to seek out only the essentials, rather than the excess. By simply asking yourself this question, you'll be amazed at what you're able to find out about yourself.

Chapter 3: Tips on How to Make Your Home More Hygge

Now that you have an understanding of how you can begin to cultivate a mindset that is largely hygge in nature, we will now turn our attention towards how you can go about turning your most intimate personal spaces into hygge-rich environments. This chapter is going to discuss hygge home decorating trends. After reading this chapter, you will have a perfect understanding the types of interior design techniques that you can bring into your home in order to provide your home with a comfier and all around cozier feeling. Let's take a look at how you can make your home hygge in ways that are as easy to implement as they are incredibly cozy and relaxing.

Interior Styling Tip 1: Light Your Home Appropriately

Both candles and fireplaces can be defined as two key aspects of the hygge lighting aesthetic. Candles are a huge aesthetic aspect of designing a hygge space. Even if you do not own a fireplace, thinking about how you can create lighting in your home in a way that connotes a feeling of warmness and glowing quality is a great way to start creating more of a hyggelig environment (hyggelig is an adjective form of the word hygge). If you're looking to make the lighting in your home more hygge, you should be looking to obtain a golden hue in your space. This type of color is usually naturally derived from the light that candles and fireplaces are able to contribute to a room. Types of artificial light that can bring more of a golden color to a room include the light that comes from vintage bulbs as well as light bulbs that are a lower wattage than a 100-watt bulb.

It's important to understand that while golden light is going to produce an all-around cozier feeling, there are some other advantages that also exist when you're able to introduce more golden lighting into your environment. For example, from a psychological perspective it's known that dimmer lighting can cause people to be in a better mood than they otherwise would be under normal lighting conditions. Additionally, people are usually better to communicate when the lighting is warmer and it's been also proven that they're able to think in a more creative capacity. Lastly, there has been some research done that suggests that when you spend time gazing at a fire, what you're essentially doing is relaxing your mind. All of these factors combine to produce the enhanced cozy feeling that hygge advocates.

Interior Styling Tip 2: Make Yourself a "Hyggekrog"

Another interior design look to consider that will nicely coincide with your desire to be more hygge involves creating what's known as a hyggekrog. In English, a hyggekrog would probably best be defined as a nook or some other type of relaxing space where you can unwind. Ideally, a hyggekrog is going to be located near a window, and will include cushions on the seats of the nook as well. Additionally, this nook space may be surrounded by bookcases, and may even be a place where you house a throw pillow or two and a blanket for your enjoyment. Finish off this space with a small table that can house some hearty snacks while you read or gaze out the window, and you'll be good to go. It's important to note that having a window for your hyggekrog is not essential. If you don't have a good window where you could set up this type of cozy environment for yourself, you can still create one from the layout that feels most appropriate for your individual space.

Interior Styling Tip 3: Make Your Bed a Lounger's Paradise

On the weekends, do you ever have the days when you feel like you don't want to get out of bed? For someone who is trying to make their space more hygge, he or she is going to want to make sure that their bed is fully equipped to handle the types of days when getting out of bed seems like an impossibility. The key ingredient to creating a cozier bed is to think layers. Especially if you live in a particularly cold region of the world, layers are going to make you feel not only warmer but also cozier due to the added weight that is going to be placed on the body.

Additionally, another important aspect of proper hygge bed etiquette involves making sure that you have the proper pillows. Unless you're someone who pays little attention to the finer things in life, you probably have an idea of the type of pillow that you prefer. Do you enjoy fluffy pillows that allow your head to melt into them, or do you prefer a pillow that is going to provide your head with some stiffer stability? Whatever your preference is, make sure that you have ample pillows available that are of this particular style. Lastly, another good product that you may want to consider investing in is a breakfast tray. Who doesn't love breakfast in bed?

Interior Styling Tip 4: The More Natural, the Better

Another facet of the hygge design culture involves natural elements being introduced into the home space. Specifically, the types of materials that hygge enthusiasts will tend to bring indoors include the elements of leather, wool, wood, and brick. When you introduce these elements into a space, the goal should be to create an aesthetic that is neutral and will make you feel calm while looking at it. Additionally, if you are thinking about introducing natural elements to a room, you should consider only implementing a couple of them so as not to bombard the space with contrast.

Interior Style Tip 5: Integrate Patterns or Texture

It's important that you keep the elements of the previous tip rather neutral in color and texture, because in addition to bringing natural elements into a space, another hygge tendency is to contrast this neutrality with specific textures or designs. For someone who lives in Denmark, the reality is that a lot of their winter months are going to be spent indoors. Without textures or patterns in their home that will bring some life into the space which they inhabit, their spaces would likely seem too boring over a long period of time cooped up in their home. For example, a hygge home may contain many wood elements, but may also contain one or two walls that are adorned with wallpaper with colored pineapples or fanciful animals on them. To this extent, the goal of the hygge home is to portray a feeling of both ease and playfulness simultaneously. Who ever said that playfulness could not also be relaxing?

Free Versus Expensive and Perfection through Décor

First of all, one of the key aspects of hygge design tactics that is important to understand is that you should be avoiding a completely manicured or uniform home. For example, in a hygge household this means that not all of the pillows in the living room area *must* match. Instead, perhaps your throw pillows are all different and have been chosen based on the fact that they all provide you with pleasure when you either look at them or lay on them in one way or another. While mixing and matching is okay when you're adopting hygge decorating ideals, this does not mean that free stuff is always the way to go. Remember, in addition to being cozy, hygge design is also simplistic. If you find that you're accumulating a bunch of free stuff that you're not using in an efficient manner, it's best to get rid of it. To this end, it's also important to keep in mind that free is not always the best thing regarding your decor. For someone who is looking to be more hygge, you want the coziest and most personally memorable goods filling up your home. On the other hand, being hygge doesn't have to cost a fortune either. Find your own personal balance.

Additionally, hygge is not at all about having the "perfect" space. When you are first starting to decorate, it's easy to get caught up in having good symmetry and balance throughout your home. For hygge design, a reliance on balance and symmetry is being replaced by the importance of your personal comfort. If things in your home don't match up perfectly, that's okay. The hygge lifestyle is more concerned about how you can create an environment where you will be able to feel most at home, regardless of how this environment compares to other types of homes in terms of "normalcy". This notion should excite you, because it asks you to be creative when it comes to truly making a space your own in a way that truly works for you.

Chapter 4: Prioritizing the People in Your Life Properly

What good would your hygge-decorated home be if you never had people over to entertain? A big part of the hygge way of life, in addition to being about decorating in a comfy way, also involves interacting with friends and family in a particular way. When life is busy, sometimes it can seem like we don't have much time for the people who are most important to us; however, when you start to live with hygge in mind, you may be surprised to find that suddenly you feel more mindful about prioritizing the people in your life. This chapter is going to discuss ways that you can begin to form relationships that are more hygge and less sterile or basic in nature.

Invite More People into Your Space

Once you have a home that is cozy and speaks perfectly to your personal ideals of comfort, why not share these ideals with others? If you live somewhere in the West, or in the United States, then there's a chance that you often resist the urge to invite others into your home on a regular basis. When you've created a cozy and inviting atmosphere, there should be nothing stopping you from bringing more people whom you care about spending time with into your home. While it may be initially daunting to think about having someone casually occupy your home for a long period of time, it's these types of casual interactions that will make you closer to someone. When you do end up inviting people into your hygge home, try to resist the urge to have an "agenda". Instead, simply allow things to unfold as they may.

Lurk More!

Another concept that is unique to hygge when it comes to developing better and more mindful relationships with the people around you are the idea of lurking more. This goes hand-in-hand with not setting an agenda when you invite someone over into your home. Rather than conversing with someone only to make a point or so that you can obtain the information that you need, a better approach might be to stick around after you've gotten the information that you're seeking and see how else you can connect with the person to whom you're talking. This will allow you to perhaps find out more about the person that would otherwise not be possible if you were to simply stop talking to the person after figuring out the information that you need. Another benefit of lurking is that it often allows you to better understand where the other person is coming from as well as their perspective on life. This is a humbling and simultaneously unifying experience that most Danes are good at cultivating.

Think "Hang Out" Instead of Formal Wine and Dine

Another important aspect of interacting with people in a more hygge fashion is to think about the types of gatherings you want to have. The type of gathering that you should be trying to have if you're keeping within hygge ideals should be one that is informal, casual, and cozy. For example, instead of inviting your friends over for a dinner party that will include a three-course meal of salad, entrée and dessert with copious amounts of wine, it might be a better idea to host a dinner that will include large casseroles of comfort food, beer, and any other types of libations that you know your guests love. From the perspective of hygge, there's no real point in serving food that people are not going to absolutely love. The way that you present the meal is going to have a big impact on how formal the event feels. It's important to keep this in mind as you move through the dinner planning process.

Initiate a Bonfire Hang

A bonfire can be considered to be the perfect hygge setting. Even if you don't have a bonfire of your own or know how to make one from scratch, these days it's incredibly easy to find a chimenea or outdoor fireplace at a home improvement store for a relatively cheap price. Bonfires, with their emphasis on both fire and natural elements that are used to start them, are quite hygge in nature. Additionally, a bonfire is also a casual setting that will allow you to talk intimately with your friends with few interruptions. If you don't personally own a bonfire and don't plan on purchasing one anytime soon, there might be places within the vicinity in which you live that has a bonfire that you can go to instead. Of course, these types of places are likely going to be more crowded than if you were sitting around your own personal bonfire, so you have to decide if this type of outing is worth it to you.

Perform Loving Actions

Living more of a hygge lifestyle certainly does not mean that it's necessary to be constantly inviting people into your home in order to hang out. If you are a truly busy person and don't have a lot of time to spare in terms of formally spending long periods of time with another person, you can still show the important people in your life that you care about them. Remember, friendships require upkeep in order to work, and this is why it's important to somewhat frequently reach out to the people you care about and show them how they mean a lot to you. This can be as simple as sending them an email or a handwritten letter, or it could be as complex as sending them a gift through the mail. Remember, hygge is all about the little things, which is why this type of gesture can go a long way from a friend point of view.

Start a New Hygge-Inspired Tradition

Another way that you can spend more time around the people whom you care about and create new memories at the same time involves starting a new tradition. The word "tradition" can be a bit misleading, because it is usually used when discussing holidays or special events. In reality, a tradition can be as simple as hosting a monthly game night at your house, or planning an activity that you and your friends are going to participate in once a year. In this way, you are planning for a good time in the future, which can often keep the people in your life excited and eager to spend time with you and your closest pals. By creating something that is "special", you're essentially making it more likely that the people with whom you're closest are going to be around now and far into the future.

Chapter 5: Finding the Food and Hygge Balance

By now, you should be able to see that there are hygge ideals that can be obtained for almost any aspect of your life, including food. This chapter is going to focus on the types of foods that you can enjoy that will certainly leave you feeling cozy, satisfied, and happy. After reading this chapter, not only will you have a better understanding of the types of foods that you should be consuming in order to feel hygge yourself; you'll also have developed a strong knowledge of how to interact with food in a way that will leave the people around you feeling loved and happy as well.

Making It Yourself Versus Buying It in the Store

One of the first important points to recognize about food in a hygge home is that a lot of the food that is consumed should be food that has been prepared by you or by someone with whom you live. Yes, baking hearty goods for your entire household often takes a lot of time, but the goal when you're cooking hygge food is to make it mindfully, so that the person who is consuming it is able to taste the love and effort that you've put into it in every bite. From the perspective of hygge, it's not considered lazy to purchase goods in the store; obviously, some food is better off being bought rather than made yourself. A big reason why the hygge foods that we're going to discuss should be made from scratch, when possible, is because of the delicious smells that these foods can bring into your home. Similar to the cozy feeling you can get when cookies are baking in the oven, hygge definitely advocates for cooking and baking foods that will leave your house smelling hearty and wonderful.

Foods that Are Considered Hygge

Now that you know what the major benefits are in terms of cooking and baking your own hygge food, now it is time to look at some of the specific types of foods that you can make if you want to embody hygge ideals in the kitchen. Remember, hygge is about mindfulness. This means that even if you end up botching the recipe that you're working on, it's important to find content in the actual process of making the food in question. If you can't find personal enjoyment in the activity itself, you're not deriving the hygge essence from the activity in question. Let's take a look at some of the most popular hygge foods so that you can get them into your kitchen as quickly as possible.

Hygge Food 1: Cinnamon Buns

If you've ever gone to a bakery or even a Dunkin Donuts to purchase a donut or a muffin with your coffee in the morning, then you already know how purchasing this type of treat can feel. When you make cinnamon buns at home, this feeling is enhanced because you've made these delicacies yourself. Even if you made your cinnamon buns ahead of time and reheat them for breakfast during the week, drinking your morning coffee with a homemade cinnamon bun in hand will likely relax you and provide you with a great start to your morning.

Hygge Food 2: Smorrebrod

You don't have to use these Danish terms in your own everyday language, but they're fun to try to pronounce nonetheless! Smorrebrod can loosely be translated to mean "stuff on toast". Remember, being hygge is certainly not about finding perfection in your life, but it is about having a certain level of simplicity to it. We don't always have the perfect ingredients in the home. Sometimes, we have to work with what we've got. That's what the notion of smorrebrod is all about. Avocado, hard boiled eggs, cream cheese, and even your favorite sliced up vegetables are all great ways that you can spice up a piece of boring old toast.

Hygge Food 3: Swedish Meatballs

If you have ever gone shopping at Ikea, then you should already know that a key feature of any Ikea outing involves dining at their cafeteria and indulging in some Swedish meatballs after a long day of furniture shopping. These types of meatballs offer a sweeter flavor than a regular Italian meatball, and can easily be consumed with other hearty foods such as potatoes and gravy. My mouth is starting to water just thinking about how delicious this type of comfort food would be on a cloudy and cold evening.

Hygge Food 4: Stew or Chili

Another great comfort food that can be considered hygge in nature are stews and chilis. As long as you have a slow cooker or have room on your stove for a large pot to simmer for long hours on end, you're going to be able to experience the delicious smells that will emanate from a stew or chili dish. What's also great about this type of meal is that it can serve a lot of people and it is relatively easy to make and maintain. A stew or a chili could be the perfect dinner to make while you're hosting a game night or another type of casual gathering at your house. This way, there will be pleasant aromas wafting through your house all evening, and you won't have all that much actual cooking to do.

Hygge Food 5: Soup

Making a hearty soup for yourself and for your loved ones is extremely hygge in nature. There's nothing like a warm and indulgent soup to eat while you're curled up on the couch watching a movie with a friend or a significant other. It's important to note here that some soups are better than others. The best advice is to start simple if you've never made soup before. For example, I know someone who had little experience with cooking soup, but he wanted to try it. He decided to try and make celery root soup, and it turned out to be a disaster. He had never cooked with celery root before, and the flavor of the soup ended up being metallic, too acidic, and to put it bluntly awful. Some easy soups that you should try to make prior to making anything complicated include tomato soup, potato and corn chowder, or butternut squash soup with bacon.

Hygge Food Type 6: Bread

Another major food group that is a part of any serious hygge diet is bread. Cooking bread inside of your home is going to produce a lovely aroma that is unmatched in terms of coziness. Additionally, another great hygge idea that you can use for your own indulgency involves making your own soup and your own bread at the same time. Of course, the amount of work that this type of cooking endeavor requires should not be taken lightly. Bread in particular can be rather difficult to make, especially if you are not using a bread kit and are instead looking to completely make this bread from scratch. In order to make bread, you are going to need to possess a lot of patience, because bread can easily go from appearing to be rising nicely to looking like a pancake or a wafer. Take your time, and understand that bread making requires great attention to detail and accuracy. This will allow you to make bread while starting on the right foot.

Hygge Food Type 7: Eat More Porridge

Porridge is a word that you don't often hear if you live in the United States; however, for a Danish person, porridge could almost be considered to be a staple food of their diet. Oatmeal is quite similar to porridge, but it's important to understand that oatmeal is often defined as a *type* of porridge that exists within the porridge family. While oatmeal is almost always made with some type of grain, porridge can be made with vegetables or even legumes in some cases. Porridge is a comfort food in the sense that it is almost always served hot, and there are many varieties of porridge that you can consume. In this way, it's safe to say that porridge is similar to the smorrebrod that we've already discussed. If you're creative, you should be able to concoct a porridge meal from simple and diverse ingredients in your home.

Hygge Foods and Your Diet

Even though hygge is all about being indulgent, cozy and eating comfort food, it's important to note that this does not mean that you should go insane with the amount of comfort food that you're eating on a daily basis. As with any diet, variety is important, especially from a health perspective. Of course, we are all probably excited about the fact that a major part of the hygge diet seems to revolve around bread; however, this does not mean that this book is advocating for daily consumption of many slices of bread. In fact, hygge is as much as mindfulness as it is about indulgence and comfort. It's unlikely that you feel comfortable in your own body if you're plumping yourself up by consuming comfort foods on a daily basis. When your health is on the line, it's crucial that you understand your own body's limits, so that you don't end up getting fat or sick. It's that simple. The bottom line is, use your discretion when cooking and consuming heavy levels of carbohydrates and comfort food.

Chapter 6: Indulging and Investing in Yourself

Now that you know what types of food you should be cooking when you want to be hygge, this next chapter is going to focus on the types of activities you can do in order to enjoy these foods while you hygge out. Remember, one of the major reasons why the Danes are so good at entertaining themselves through simple pleasures is because they spend a lot of their time in darkness during the winter months. For this reason, self-entertainment is almost essential for someone who is living in Denmark. The result of this need for self-entertainment is happiness, because the Danes are able to find and derive pleasure from hobbies that may be considered "boring" to someone who is constantly finding new avenues for entertainment. The hobbies listed in this chapter are important because once you start to learn how to entertain yourself and feel pleasure in spending some time alone, happiness should be quite easy to obtain.

Additionally, there is sometimes a tendency in Western society to be constantly "doing" something. You may find that when you're alone and have nothing to do, you're suddenly bored or uninterested in life. This is perhaps the wrong way to be living. If you can slowly start to spend longer amounts of time by yourself, doing an activity that is personally pleasing to you, you may find that you're suddenly finding out new things about yourself that you previously did not know or understand. Spending time alone can be therapeutic, yet people in Western society often shy away from it. Perhaps this is because spending time alone won't look fabulous in a social media photo, or because there are so many sources of entertainment these days that it can sometimes seem pointless to do anything by yourself. To make this more concrete, below is a list of benefits that come with spending time alone:

1. **Increases Productivity:** Spending time alone allows you to relax and truly be yourself in a way that is arguably not possible, even when the person who is around is someone who you trust and love. By taking time out of your day to spend time alone and regroup, you're allowing the brain to recharge and prepare for the next time it has to work and be productive.
2. **Establishes Your Voice:** Have you ever been around a friend who is particularly domineering? Whenever you're in a group setting, you're opening yourself up to being coerced into thinking and making decisions based on whatever the group consensus is at the time. When you spend time alone, the truth of the matter is that you get to know yourself better than you do when you're being influenced by other people. This is especially going to be true if you're someone who is typically shy or have a more "go with the flow" personality. Additionally, people often like people more who have their own opinion on things. In this way, spending more time alone will allow you to feel more confident when it comes time to making your first heard in social situations.
3. **Allows for More Effective Problem Solving:** Lastly, another reason why spending time alone can be cathartic is because it can help you to solve problems in a more effective manner. Whether it be the people around you who are trying to influence the way that you go about solving a problem, or it's the digital media that may be influencing you, the best way to solve a problem is often by thinking it through on your own. At the end of the day, you have to live with the decisions that you're making, so by spending time alone you're able to truly think through any type of problem that you may be having.

Take Up Knitting or Crocheting

One hobby that will most likely allow you to feel relaxed, concentrated, and inspired all at the same time involves taking up knitting or crocheting. It can be argued that learning how to crochet is easier than learning how to knit, because crocheting only involves using one tool while knitting involves using two tools. This being the case, the best advice is to start taking up crocheting and then work towards learning how to knit. If you know someone who already understands how to do one of these hobbies, then you may want to reach out to him or her and see if they will agree to provide you with some pointers. Once you get the hang of either activity that you choose, you're likely going to enjoy the hobby because it will allow you to concentrate on the task at hand as well as easily see the progress that you're making over a short period of time. Even if you start simple, what one day will look like a piece of string will suddenly turn into a beautiful blanket or a scarf in no time at all.

Meditate

Another great way to truly find inner peace and contentment is through meditation. Meditation allows you to slow down, and can also help you to see things more objectively than they otherwise may seem. A great application that can help you get more into meditating is known as headspace. This application walks you through meditation by increasing the length of time that you spend meditating over the course of a week as well as guiding you through the meditation with a peaceful and soothing instructor. Everyone has five minutes that they can spend meditating, and meditation can be a great way to truly turn inward and slow down the busy thoughts that you may be having throughout the day. In this way, meditation is able to provide an individual with a tremendous amount of clarity and relaxation, especially after a particularly long or stressful day.

Read a Book Series

If you love to read and are looking to become more consistent in reading on a regular basis, you can challenge yourself to start reading a popular book series. When you read a book that is not in a series, you're able to fall in love with the characters, but once the book is over you can't get your fix of these characters and their particular plotlines anymore. This is where a book series differs from a single book that is written on its own. As long as the series is good, you'll likely want to read all of the books that are in it. Investing in a book series will help you to spend less time mindlessly watching television or binging on Netflix. Instead, you'll be able to spend time alone with your thoughts and with the characters in the book series as well.

Declutter

Perhaps you're someone who knows that clutter is one of your weaknesses. Your house is filled with stuff that you may need one day in the future, but that you haven't actually touched in a number of months or years. If you're a particularly unorganized person, there are still steps that you can take to declutter your home and your life little by little. For example, you could consider throwing out five things that you don't truly need every day for a week. If this seems too daunting, you could instead decide that you're going to give five articles of clothing to Goodwill or to another type of charity. Sometimes, when you decide that you're going to give your stuff to a better cause instead of simply throwing it away, the reality sets in that your stuff would maybe be more useful if it wasn't sitting idly in your house and was instead being used by someone who truly needs it more than you do.

Turn Daily Activities into Rituals

Lastly, being more indulgent in regards to yourself can also involve treating the daily things that you do in a way that is more ritualistic in nature. For example, instead of simply taking a shower on a weeknight, why not take the time to shower yourself in some indulgence and prepare for a bath instead? This bath could include the purchasing of candles, your favorite bottle of wine, and maybe even a good book or a playlist of your favorite soothing music. If you think baths are gross and you'd rather not take one, you can still pamper yourself in other ways. Purchasing a fancy foot cream or a face mask are two other types of treats in which you can indulge that will turn your typical evening into something that is just a little bit more special.

Additionally, it's important to note here that it is quite hygge to invest in spa days or spa treatments of any type. These types of treatments can range from getting a massage to going to the gym and spending a long period of time in the sauna or hot tub. These treatments, while often luxurious, can also often come with a price tag that is not desirable for some. If you're someone who would rather not spend a load of money on a spa treatment, you can always opt to take the spa treatment into your own hands. Giving yourself a manicure or even taking some time to think about how you can make your wardrobe more creative are both ways that you can spend some time pampering and improving the way that you feel and look.

Chapter 7: Activities with Friends that Are So Hygge it Hurts

While the previous chapter documented what you can do while you have alone time, it's safe to say that there can come a point when too much alone time is not a good thing. This chapter will talk about activities that you can perform with your friends that go beyond hosting a dinner party or having a game night at your house. We don't all live in a place where winter seems to be the season that is the most prevalent, but that doesn't mean that hygge ideals cannot be attainable. Let's take a look at some of the activities that you can do with others in both a friendship capacity as well as in a capacity that will help you to become more integrated in your community.

Go Camping

One of the best ways to engage and invest in the elements that surround you in life is to go camping with your friends. Once you're in the natural elements, there are plenty of activities that you can do that will make your time in nature seem both fulfilling and entertaining at the same time. For example, you can go hiking, fishing, and even take a stab at building your own campfire if you feel so inclined. It's important to note here that the advice to go camping does not imply that you should spend the majority of your time at the campsite drinking. Sure, drinking can be a fine activity to do with friends, but hygge is about experiencing life naturally, rather than through the lens of a drunken stupor.

Sweater Swap

Another great way that you can get more involved with your community and not just with the friends that you currently have is to initiate some sort of sweater swap in your community. Of course, if you live in a place that generally experiences a warmer climate throughout the year, a sweater swap may not be appropriate; however, you can always change the article of clothing in question so that it better fits with the season in which you're planning to do the swap. Additionally, if you're coordinating this activity, it would probably a good idea to ensure everyone that you are personally going to be washing the clothes so that everything is truly clean prior to the swap event. After everything is clean, you'll also want to expect each item of clothing in question to make sure that all of the clothing matches in terms of quality.

Consider Taking Up a New Group Hobby

Another way that you can spend more time with the people in your life is to take up a new hobby with them. For example, if you live in a place where there is a lot of beautiful nature, why not get a group together to go on weekly hikes with each other, or find a few people who will try a new sport workout activity with you. Along these same lines, it's important to understand that hygge involves thinking about exercising in general a bit differently than you may currently be used to doing. Instead of thinking about working out as an activity that will ultimately lead to great results for your body, hygge ideals advocate for exercise to be more leisure and less productive. For example, if you're going to the gym, why not simply do activities that make you feel good, rather than perform an activity simply because it will result in a physical benefit but is rather unpleasant to perform itself. The *process* of the sport should be as pleasurable as the results that will come from it.

Rent a Dog for the Day

If you do not currently own a dog, another option that you have that would be fun to do with friends is to rent a dog for a day. What is cozier than cuddling up with a dog in the park or on the beach? When you do this with other people, you're all able to share in the joy of hanging out with a cute and cuddly animal for at least a day or two. Plus, when you decide to partake in this type of activity with friends, you're also able to bring the cost of doing this down. On average, renting a dog on a weekend day is going to cost you around forty dollars for the day. On a weekday, borrowing a dog will only cost around twenty-five dollars, but it's more likely that you would be borrowing a dog on the weekend and not during the week.

If you already own a dog, you can still spend time with your dog and others all at the same time. Remember, hygge is all about showing the people in your life that you care about them. When you own a pet, you can also extend this notion to your animal. Your animal needs just as much, if not more, recognition of the fact that you love them on a frequent basis. Additionally, bringing your dog or other type of pet around people who you trust and care about can be an enjoyable thing for both the animal and friends who are involved.

Go Ice Skating

This next activity is pretty winter-like in nature, for the simple fact that you're not going to be able to go ice skating if you live in a place where all of the ice is going to melt. Ice skating is considered to be a hygge activity for a few different reasons. Firstly, you have to dress in a cozy way when you ice skate so that you don't freeze while you're on the ice. Secondly, ice skating often brings with it warm drinks such as hot cocoa or coffee, which are also hygge-like drinks. Lastly, ice skating is an activity that is both active and enjoyable at the same time (unless you're someone who falls on the ice more than you skate on the ice). If you live in a place where it's often warm instead of chilly, you can still plan to partake in winter sports. Planning a ski trip with friends can be an incredibly fun and memorable time.

Take Up Yoga

These days, it seems like yoga is everywhere. If you're currently someone who is weirded out by the thought of doing strange poses in yoga pants or loose shorts, hear me out. Yoga often goes hand-in-hand with meditation, and can offer you a great way to turn inward and find out more about yourself than you could probably ever imagine. While yoga is largely an individual activity, it's an activity that can be done with friends at the same time. If you've never tried yoga before, then grabbing a few friends and heading to a yoga studio will likely relax some of the tension or apprehension that you may feel surrounding the activity. If yoga is something that you're willing to try with some friends, it's incredibly important that you take some time to think about the type of yoga that you want to do. As was already stated, yoga seems to be everywhere today. This means that there are many different types of yoga that's out there. Are you someone who would prefer a gentle yoga class, a class for true beginners, or an intense class that is more like a workout class in nature? If you don't choose the class that best fits your personality and individual style, you'll likely walk away from the experience feeling frustrated or bad about yourself.

Chapter 8: Hygge Fashion Tips that Will Make Your Wardrobe Pop

Now that we've discussed many activities that you can do both by yourself and with friends, this final chapter is going to discuss how you can dress yourself while you're doing these activities that are aligned with hygge principles. After you're finished reading this chapter, you should be able to combine all of the tactics that were presented in this book and begin to live by hygge ideals in a way that will lead to a comfier and most importantly happier way of life. Let's take a look at some of the hygge fashion rules that you can live by, so that your wardrobe can start to match your overall demeanor and attitude towards life in general.

Function Over Fashion

The single most important hygge wardrobe principle involves thinking about fashion in a way that is primarily practical. This largely has to do with matching your wardrobe with the type of environment in which you find yourself during any given event or point in time. For example, if you've ever been to college in a location where the climate is cold, then you know that there are many girls who choose to go out on the weekends in skimpy dresses and short skirts in the freezing cold without a jacket or a coat on. These girls are not in any way shape or form living with hygge in mind. If these girls were to adhere to hygge ideals, it would mean that instead of wearing these dresses and skirts that are barely there, they'd be wearing heavy clothing that leaves them feeling comfy and cozy. Even if you don't remember any of the other rules that were presented in this chapter, the notion of function over fashion is inherent to the entire hygge fashion culture. Of course, this doesn't mean that you have to walk around looking frumpy or ugly, but if an individual were put into a situation where he or she had to choose between being cold in a pretty spaghetti-strap dress or being warm in a wool dress that looked like a potato sack, a true hygge enthusiast would choose the potato sack every time.

Think More Layers

In addition to thinking about how clothing can serve a function rather than be completely cute or pretty, another crucial aspect to understanding hygge fashion is the idea of layering your clothing as well. For example, if it's cold outside, why not consider wearing a pair of leggings or long underwear underneath the pants that you're going to wear to work? If you take the time to really think about what's going to look good from a layering perspective, there's no reason why your layering techniques can't be both cute and warm all at the same time.

Knits Are In

Because so much of hygge revolves around being warm when it's cold outside, another significant trend that has emerged in terms of hygge style has to do with knits. Let's go back to our example of the scantily-clad dressed college girl for a moment. Let's say that instead of choosing to wear a spaghetti strap dress when it is snowing outside with no jacket on, this person instead chooses to adorn herself in a dress that was entirely made of wool. This decision would be incredibly hygge in nature. Along with clothing that is entirely made of wool, another trend that's apparent within hygge fashion is fringe. The idea behind using both knits and fringe as staples of the hygge fashion movement could be because both of these types of fabric choices can be found on blankets, which are about as cozy as it gets.

Think Simple

As we've already discussed earlier in this book, an aspect of hygge involves living simply. This idea of simplicity also translates to hygge clothing, and most notably manifests itself with the color black. While an outfit that is entirely made of black clothing may seem goth or harrowing to come, an all-black outfit compliments the hygge fashion ideal quite nicely. If you're thinking about picking out an all-black outfit for yourself that exists within the hygge spectrum, you should be trying to keep in mind that the bulkier the top, the better. On the other hand, the bottoms for the outfit should be less bulky and snugger to the body.

If you completely disagree with the notion of dressing yourself in an entirely black outfit, you still have options. For example, you can still mix and match your tops and bottoms, but keep the contrast simple rather than stark. Patterned clothing should be worn to a minimum, unless you are contrasting the pattern with some type of bold and single color or design. Lastly, if you are someone who simply does not want to wear colors that are close in color or pattern, you can instead spice up your wardrobe with some kind of accessory piece or bag.

The Comfier the Socks, the Better

Another aspect of the hygge wardrobe that you're best not to do without are cozy and warm socks. Even if you're wearing a shoe that will not fit a sock that is particularly thick, you can still invest in a thin sock that will keep your foot adequately warm. These types of socks are called Merino socks. While they're not quite as warm as socks that are made of 100% wool, they're close to being as warm. Additionally, these socks are going to be able to fit into any type of boot that you're wearing, even if the boot is rather snug to your feet.

Earmuffs and Scarves

In keeping with the notion that your clothing should be functional before it's fashionable, two other essential items to have in your hygge closet are earmuffs and scarves. These days, you can easily find both earmuffs and scarves that are going to be able to match with the rest of your outfit. For scarves in particular, you should be able to also find one that will complement every season imaginable. People wear scarves in all types of climates, and the material of the scarf is going to be able to dictate how warm or how cool it will be for your neck. Earmuffs largely work in a similar manner. When it's only slightly chilly outside, fluffy earmuffs should be able to keep your ears adequately warm. On the other hand, if you're in a location where the weather is extremely cold and frigid, a hat or earmuffs that are lined with fleece may prove to be more appropriate.

Conclusion

Thank for making it through to the end of *Hygge: An Introduction to the Danish Art of Cozy Living*. Hopefully, this book has been able to serve as a source of comprehensive information regarding what the hygge lifestyle is and how it can benefit your life. Remember, you can use the information that was presented in this book to any extent that you'd like. The entire point of hygge is to use the tactics that exist within it in a way that will enhance the pleasure that you have in your life. By creating a cozy atmosphere for yourself and cultivating trust and enjoyment with the people around you, you'll be able to maximize the enjoyment that you can get out of your life, both over the short as well as the long-term.

The next step is to start integrating more hygge concepts into your life. The best idea here would be to choose the most appealing aspect of the hygge lifestyle that was presented in this book, and then work towards establishing these types of principles into your own life. It's important that while you're attempting to integrate these changes into your life that you take it at your own pace. If you move too quickly, there is always the chance that you will become overwhelmed, especially if the changes that you're looking to make are drastic. For example, if you're someone who has lived a life that is for the most part the complete opposite of hygge, then implementing a lot of hygge principles at once may ultimately make you feel overwhelmed. The best advice here is to take your time, and find pleasure in the act of changing your lifestyle tactics. This way, you're less likely to feel stressed or feel like hygge just isn't for you. Hygge is for everyone!

www.ingramcontent.com/pod-product-compliance
Lightning Source LLC
Chambersburg PA
CBHW051542020426
42333CB00016B/2051